THE
CHANGING FACE
OF AUSTRALIA

004

The Changing Face of Australia

A century of immigration
1901 - 2000

Kate Walsh

FOREWORD

There is an enormous contemporary literature, and much everyday comment and analysis, on immigration to Australia. The reason for this is not hard to find – immigration covers so many aspects of the nation's life. Almost one quarter of Australia's population were born overseas, and a further fifth are the children of parents from abroad. Consequently, more than two fifths of the present population of Australia have shared directly or closely in the experience of migration. And the remainder has been host to successive waves of new arrivals from many countries.

After Israel and Luxembourg, Australia is the most intensely immigrant country in the world: the proportion of the population born abroad is higher in Australia than anywhere else, with those two exceptions. This reflects the strength of the post World War II immigrant intake: of the ten million immigrants who have come to Australia since 1778, two thirds arrived after 1947.

Also, the long history of Australia has included, historians tell us, at least two waves of ancient migration by Australia's Indigenous Aboriginal people. They inhabited Australia for thousands of decades prior to the comparatively very recent arrival as settlers over two hundred years ago of people from the British Isles.

The book covers only a part of this extended history, and rightly refers to Aboriginal communities who were greatly affected by the new arrivals, as well as mainly to the fresh immigrants themselves. It marks the past one hundred years of Federation, during which eighty per cent of all immigrants since 1788 have arrived. Only two of the ten million immigrants arriving in Australia since 1788 came before Federation. The book seeks to show, by pictures and brief accompanying text, a collection of telling images of this segment of the broader, much longer history of immigration to Australia.

Such is the richness of the photographic heritage of the period, and the complexity of history, only a selected smidgen of the past can be shown. But that brief look is, I believe, enough to give an intriguing perspective into where the immigrants went and what their lives and experiences were over the first century of Federation.

The idea for this project was born over five years ago when the former Bureau of Immigration, Multicultural and Population Research, of which I was Director, provided funds for a celebratory history of immigration since Federation. After the Bureau's abolition in 1996, it was feared the project would falter. However, the successful tenderers, the South Australian Migration Museum, under the vigorous leadership of Viv Szekeres, gained supplementary finance from the Centenary of Federation Fund and also from CEDA, the Committee for Economic Development of Australia. The monumental task of authorship, including selecting photographs, with brief accompanying text, in an historically orderly and, as far as possible, representative way, fell to Kate Walsh, who has done an excellent job. The outcome speaks for itself. It will be a continuing source of interest to all Australians, and others in the lands from which the people came.

The principal contribution of the book, I believe, is to highlight through photos and incisive, compressed comment the images of the changing times, and the contexts within which millions of people from a multitude of lands came to call Australia home.

The Changing Face of Australia should be an enduring work, of interest to current and future generations in Australia and abroad. The volume underlines a proud feature of Australian history. In other immigrant receiving countries there has been resistance to welcoming immigrants as citizens and full members of the new society. Of such countries, it has been said that their immigrants are people of two worlds, the one half dead, the other unattainable. It is Australia's achievement, however, that for many millions of migrants in the period since Federation a new world has been successfully born.

John Nieuwenhuysen
Chief Executive, CEDA
Committee for Economic Development of Australia

This edition published in 2001

Allen & Unwin
83 Alexander Street
Crows Nest NSW 2065
Australia
Phone: (61 2) 8425 0100
Fax: (61 2) 9906 2218
Email: frontdesk@allen-unwin.com.au
Web: http://www.allenandunwin.com

National Library of Australia
Cataloguing-in-Publication entry:

Walsh, Kate.
    The changing face of Australia: a century of immigration 1901–2000.

    Includes index
    ISBN 1 86508 408 5.

    1. Immigrants—Australia—History. 2. Multiculturalism—Australia. 3. Australia—Emigration and immigration—History. I. Title.

325.94

Printed by South China Printing Co., Hong Kong

10 9 8 7 6 5 4 3 2 1

CONTENTS

**Published by
Allen & Unwin**

A Migration Museum project

*The Migration Museum is a museum of
the History Trust of South Australia*

The Changing Face of Australia
was generously supported by:

Commonwealth
Department of
Immigration and
Multicultural Affairs

National Council
for the Centenary of
Federation, History and
Education Program

Committee for Economic
Development of Australia

Half-title page photograph: Certificate exempting
from dictation test for Go Gee, Sydney, 1908. National
Archives of Australia. (Detail)

Title page photograph: Passport photograph of Frank
Manicola who arrived in Australia from Malta in 1924.
La Trobe Picture Collection, State Library of Victoria
832880.

INTRODUCTION

This is a story, told in photographs, of immigrants who arrived and settled in Australia during the twentieth century.

It tells the story of those who came from many places and left their mark on Australia's landscape, cities, industries and cultural life.

At key moments, the story acknowledges the impact that immigrants have had, and continue to have, on Indigenous Australians.

Five hundred photographs were chosen from collections held in libraries, archives, historical societies, museums, government agencies and community clubs around Australia. Others came from family albums, their inclusion making the point that personal photographs can effectively assist in the interpretation of historical events and add to our understanding of the social context of past decades.

Many photographs pose more questions than they answer. The intent of the photographer is not always known. With some images only the briefest of information about the historical, community or personal context has been retained. People may also misremember the past and photographs can be inaccurately, as well as inadequately, captioned.

Immigrants have photographed celebrations, achievements and reunions more often than they have recorded the moments of loss, pain, difficulty, alienation or discrimination that have also been a part of their experience. Governments have tended to focus on the milestones and positive outcomes of their immigration programs.

The photographs range from the early decades of the century when there were fewer cameras, when photography was generally the preserve of the professional photographer and technology and social conventions dictated the style of images, to later decades when everyone owned a camera. Then there is an overwhelming array of images, formal and informal, as families and organisations recorded gatherings, meetings, special occasions and events with the ubiquitous camera.

The Changing Face of Australia reveals some of the moments and issues in Australia's 20th century immigration and settlement experience, at a government, community, family and personal level.

Kate Walsh, curator
Migration Museum, Adelaide, South Australia

January 2000

The Photographs

Sources of photographs

The photographs used in *The Changing Face of Australia* have come from collections held in libraries, archives, government agencies, historical societies, museums, newspaper archives, community organisations and migrant resource centres around Australia. The two main sources of photographs were the collections of the Department of Immigration and Multicultural Affairs in Canberra and the Migration Museum in Adelaide. I thank the staff of the organisations listed below for their enthusiasm, goodwill and efficient assistance given to me during this project.

Much of the photographic record which contributes to our understanding of Australia's social, and in particular, immigration history, is held by families and individuals. I thank the people listed below. They allowed me to copy their personal photographs. They shared their stories with me.

South Australia

Migration Museum

History Trust of South Australia

Lutheran Archives

The Advertiser

United Trades & Labor Council of S.A.

Mortlock Library of South Australiana, State Library of South Australia

South Australian Museum

Office of Multicultural and International Affairs

English Language and Literacy Services, Adelaide Institute of TAFE

Cornish Association of South Australia

Federation of Ethnic Communities Councils of Australia

John and Marie Boland, Shelley Huxley, Koula Aslanidis, Mark Pharoah, Peter Cahalan, Rosa Garcia, Isabel and Peter Hasse, the Spinelli family, Derek and Alice Taylor, Martin Deckys and George Donikian

Australian Capital Territory

Department of Immigration and Multicultural Affairs (DIMA)

National Library of Australia

Australian Institute of Aboriginal and Torres Strait Islander Studies (AIATSIS)

National Archives of Australia

Dr Barry York

Northern Territory

Chung Wah Society Historical Museum

Paspaley Pearls

Migrant Resource Centre of Central Australia

Vietnamese Association of the Northern Territory

Museum and Art Gallery of the Northern Territory

Glenys Dimond and Hector Farreras

Victoria

La Trobe Picture Collection, State Library of Victoria

Jewish Museum of Australia

Italian Historical Society

Chinese Museum of Australia

National Archives of Australia, Melbourne office

Princes Hill Primary School

Textile, Clothing and Footwear Union of Australia

Leslie and Joyce Lester

New South Wales

State Library of New South Wales

National Archives of Australia, Sydney office

Macleay Museum, University of Sydney

Musica Viva Australia

Richmond River Historical Society

NSW Council of Turkish Associations

Wollongong Turkish Society Inc

Botany Migrant Resource Centre

Hunter's Hill Historical Society

Local Studies Unit, Mona Vale Library

Auburn Turkish Islamic Cultural Centre

Fairfield Adult Migrant Education Service

Wollongong District Finnish Society

Anglicare

African Communities Council of NSW

Australian Romanian Association

The Sydney Morning Herald/John Fairfax & Sons

Alfredo Goldbach and Sandra de Souza

Western Australia

Battye Library, Library Information Service of Western Australia

City of Belmont Historical Society

Augusta Historical Museum

Busselton Historical Society

Denmark Historical Society

Queensland

John Oxley Library, State Library of Queensland

Innisfail and District Historical Society

Brisbane Migrant Resource Centre

Tasmania

Launceston City Library

Queen Victoria Museum & Art Gallery

The Mercury

State Library of Tasmania

Czechoslovakian Association of Tasmania

Kumi Barnes

Acknowledgements

I thank the following people who have in various ways assisted me in the compilation of the photographs for *The Changing Face of Australia* since I commenced work on the project in 1995.

Reference group

The following people generously gave their time to act as a reference group. I am indebted to them for their suggestions and criticisms of the drafts, their enthusiastic participation at meetings and for their constant support and commitment to the project.

Mr John Nieuwenhuysen
CEO
Committee for Economic Development of Australia (CEDA)

Mr John Iremonger
Academic Publishing Editor
Allen & Unwin

Dr Peter Cahalan
Director
History Trust of South Australia

Dr Sev Ozdowski
CEO
Office of Multicultural and International Affairs,
South Australian Department of Premier and Cabinet

Mr Glen Smith
State Director (SA)
Department of Immigration and Multicultural Affairs

The Hon Jennifer Cashmore

The Hon Anne Levy

Dr Robert Nicol
State Historian
History Trust of South Australia

Ms Viv Szekeres
Director
Migration Museum

Ms Rosa Garcia
Education Officer
Migration Museum

I thank the following historians who also read and commented on the text:

Dr James Jupp
Director
Centre for Immigration and Multicultural Studies,
Australian National University, Canberra

Professor Eric Richards
Department of History
Flinders University of South Australia

Many other people around Australia assisted me in my research, in locating photographs and in ascertaining copyright and granting permission for me to publish. I have listed as many names as possible. I know, however, that behind the scenes there were others whose names I did not know and I thank them, too.

I also thank my family and friends for their support and encouragement.

South Australia

Migration Museum staff including Alison Fowler, Rebecca Rudzinski, Jessamy Hunt, Christine Finnimore, Bill Seager, Jean Morris and Marg Degotardi

Sev Ozdowski, Office of Multicultural and International Affairs

Randolph Alwis, Federation of Ethnic Communities Councils of Australia

Adele Pring, Aboriginal Education Unit, SA Department of Education, Training and Employment

Lynn Drew, Frank McDonnell and Geoff Speirs, History Trust of South Australia

Black and White Photographics and Atkins Technicolour

Ron Cortvriend, *The Advertiser*

Elliott Staiff

Elizabeth Walsh

Bill Versteegh

Max Fenner

Kathy Stevens, ELLS, Adelaide TAFE

Josie Kent, Returned Services League

Staff of the Migrant Resource Centre, Adelaide

Jonathon Melville

Enid Netting, National Archives of Australia

Ros Paterson and Diana Hancock, Cornish Association of South Australia

Lyall Kupke, Lutheran Archives

Barbara Holbourn, State Library of South Australia

Kate Alport, South Australian Museum

The Hon Carmel Zollo and Daniella Costa

Frank Barbaro, FILEF

Australian Capital Territory

Maria Green and other staff in Public Relations, DIMA

Marisa Vearing, Maxine Grant, Mignon Harvy and Maren Child, DIMA library

Wizard Personnel and Office Services and Emma Aschenberger

AusInfo

The Black and White Lab

Chris Ryan, Council for Aboriginal Reconciliation

Nevada Glenbar, AIATSIS

Wendy Morrow, Kay Nicholls and Sylvia Carr, National Library of Australia

Anne Liddell, Kathy Ho, Jill Caldwell, Stephanie Boyle and Linda MacFarlane, National Archives of Australia

Ian McShane, National Museum of Australia

Victoria

Lesleyanne Hawthorne and Lois Foster, Bureau of Immigration, Multicultural and Population Research

Dianne Reilly, Mary Lewis, Olga Tsara and Kirstie McRobert, State Library of Victoria

Helen Light, Sandy Khazam and Susan Fraine, Jewish Museum of Australia

Paul McGregor, Chinese Museum of Australia

Laura Mecca and Maria Tence, Italian Historical Society

Anna Malgorzewicz, Immigration Museum, Melbourne

Richard Gillespie and Moya McFadzean, Museum of Victoria

Ilana Paris, Dandenong/Heritage Hill Local History Centre

Annie Delaney, Textile, Clothing and Footwear Union

Maree Centofanti, Princes Hill Primary School

Tom Vollmer and Mark Brennan, National Archives of Australia

Wolfgang Sievers

Northern Territory

Glenys Dimond, history and museum consultant

Hector Farreras

Alison Warwick, Paspaley Pearls

Leony Bowey, Migrant Resource Centre of Central Australia

Bac Lam, Vietnamese Association NT

Amanda McLean, Alice Springs City Library

Katherine Public Library

Katherine branch of the National Trust

Ethnic Communities Council of the Northern Territory

Anglicare

Mahomet Beyan

Chi and Ratchanee Warawitya

Frank Que Noy

Louisa Ferriera

Joan Fong

Adam Lowe

New South Wales

Linda Brainwood, Kevin Leamon and Jennifer Broomhead, State Library of New South Wales

Elizabeth Britton, Fairfield AMES

Ivana Puren, Hunters Hill Museum and Historical Society

Veronica Dematris, Botany Migrant Resource Centre

Virginia McLeod, Local Studies Unit, Mona Vale Library

Marjatta Jukkola, Wollongong District Finnish Society

David Colville, Christine Wright and Stephen Schafer, Musica Viva Australia

Warren Kinston

Morris Monsour, African Communities of New South Wales

Mihai Maghiaru, Romanian Association of New South Wales

Annette Potts and Geoff Foley, Richmond River Historical Society

Vivian Varela, Manly, Warringah and Pittwater Historical Society

J McCarthy, Illawarra Historical Society

Rosa Loria, Botany Multicultural Resource Centre

Grace Wong, Anglicare

Musafer Orel, Council of Turkish Associations of NSW

Cengiz Erginli, Wollongong Turkish Society

Shirley Mahoney, National Archives of Australia

Elisabeth Edwards, Orange

Mr Mortimer, for the estate of Henry Talbot

Berta Cunico

Matt Slavich

Geoff Barker, Macleay Museum, University of Sydney

Mrs V J Smith, Queanbeyan and District Historical Museum Society

Staff of the Fairfax Photo Library

Colonial Limited

Western Australia

Julie Martin and Carl Studd, Battye Library

Ann Spalding, City of Belmont Historical Society and Museum

Jeannette Antoinette, the Daws family and Peg Parkin

Alan Kinson, Augusta Historical Museum

Hilda Lord, Busselton Historical Society

Malcolm Traill, Albany Public Library and Information Service

David Drakes and Laura Hamilton, Denmark Historical Society

David Taylor, *The West Australian*

Queensland

Jane Meadows, Angelo Commino and other staff, John Oxley Library

Mary Scalora, Dante Alighieri Society, Orsetto and Torrisi families, Stanthorpe

A. Martinuzzi, Innisfail Historical Society

Wendy Dixon, Shire of Landsborough Historical Society

Rita Prasad Ildes, Brisbane Migrant Resource Centre

Tasmania

Jill Cassidy, Rhonda Hamilton, Elspeth Wishart, Ross Smith, Queen Victoria Museum and Art Gallery

Judy Hollingsworth and Marianne Sargent, Launceston City Library

Josef Gala, Czechoslovakian Association of Tasmania

Grazina Smith, Ethnic Communities Council of Tasmania

Janet Weaving, *The Mercury*

1901

A NEW NATION

A new year, a new century, a new nation

1901 is a fitting date to begin to chart the role of immigrants in the development of the Australian nation in the 20th century. Not only was it the first year of the new century, it was also the year when the new Commonwealth of Australia enacted its first laws on immigration to ensure that future settlers in the new nation would maintain and reinforce the Anglo-Celtic character of the Australian people.

Over three and a half million people lived in Australia at the turn of the century. The vast majority of them were of British or Irish origin. Federation was not an act of independence from Britain, the 'Mother Country'. Australia remained a part of the British Empire and Australians continued to be British subjects. Australia's new federal system of government, the policies it set and its relationships with other countries were inextricably bound to the British Imperial government.

Australians celebrated Federation with banquets, bonfires and fireworks. There were concerts, sports days and parades. There were patriotic songs, poetry and speeches.

Official functions at the state and local level abounded. In White Cliffs (NSW) some of the locals celebrated with a bush picnic at Bunker Creek near Whipstick Station. The Union Jack on the flags they gathered in front of signalled the British origins of the Australian people.

On 1 January 1901 the six separate colonies of New South Wales, Victoria, Queensland, Tasmania, South Australia and Western Australia became one nation, the Commonwealth of Australia. The chosen form of union was a federation, with the Commonwealth and the colonies, now called states, sharing the powers and responsibilities of government.

The majority of Australians in a majority of colonies voted for Federation in a referendum in 1899, after an earlier referendum in 1898 had failed to secure the required votes. This successful vote came after years of intense debate and negotiation on the draft constitution in the colonial parliaments and at intercolonial meetings and conventions.

Western Australia voted separately in July 1900 to join the Federation.

In 1899 Sydney residents crowded outside *The Sydney Morning Herald*'s office to watch the poll results for the referendum on Federation. They were part of the generations of British settlers who had arrived from England, Scotland, Wales and from Ireland, settling across the Australian continent since 1788 when the first colony, New South Wales, was established. Although the older adults in the crowd were most probably born overseas, by the end of the 19th century, they were outnumbered by their Australian-born children and grandchildren.

In the 19th century British and Irish settlers had formed and dominated complex, diverse and changing societies in the six colonies. They had developed legal, civil and political systems. They had brought with them their British pastimes and cultural pursuits and a diversity of Christian religious practices. They had established newspapers, hospitals, schools and universities, banks, businesses, mines and factories. They had developed the sheep, cattle and wheat industries and exported goods to British markets. They had constructed a network of cities and towns, railways, roads, bridges, fences and dams, creating an infrastructure that supported a growing and mobile population. They had brought with them different attitudes about class and the roles of men and women, about workers and bosses, about the poor and charity, about race and racial superiority. These generations of immigrants had interacted with each other and the landscape to create a society that was different from and yet familiar to the one they had left behind in Britain and Ireland.

At the time of Federation, as if to emphasise the limits of
Australia's new nationhood, Australian soldiers were fighting
in an Empire war.

These Western Australian troops were among
a force of sixteen thousand men who had
volunteered as loyal British subjects to fight in
the Boer War in South Africa. Five hundred
were to lose their lives there between 1899
and 1902.

The death of Queen Victoria on 22 January
1901 plunged the new nation into mourning.
The citizens of Adelaide laid wreaths at her
statue draped in black. Around the nation a
sombre atmosphere replaced the celebrations
for the new Commonwealth.

'Australia for the Australians'

It was widely accepted across Australia that the new Australian nation would remain a loyal member of the British Empire. Supporters of an Australian republic were enthusiastic but small in number.

Members of the Australian Natives Association (ANA) endorsed Australia's position within the Empire. The flags and dresses of these members at a ball in Boulder (WA) in the early years of the new century combined the symbols of Britain and Australia. On their blouses they wore the Southern Cross, the symbol of the land of their birth. On their skirts they wore the Union Jack, the flag of the 'Mother Country', Britain.

Only Australian-born could belong to the ANA, a society formed in the early 1870s. It had nearly seventeen thousand members by 1900, mostly young men from the lower middle classes. They had rising aspirations for themselves and for their country's position within the Empire.

Their motto was 'Australia for the Australians'. They were actively involved in the movement towards Federation and opposed non-European immigration.

On the fringes of Federation

The Indigenous people of the Australian continent were excluded from the new nation. They were outsiders in their own land.

White settlement since 1788 had inflicted vast changes on Aboriginal culture and society. With Federation, British Australians reinforced their claim on the continent.

Before Federation, Aboriginal people had the right to vote in all the colonies except Western Australia and Queensland. This right was rarely exercised. Laura Harris was one of the Aboriginal people at Point McLeay, a settlement near the mouth of the River Murray in South Australia, who were on the electoral roll and voted in elections. After Federation, debate ensued for decades as to whether Aboriginal people could vote in Commonwealth elections because of their previous state rights. Legal opinion varied and over time Commonwealth bureaucrats disqualified Aboriginal people, such as Laura, from enrolment. It was 1949 before those who previously had voting rights in their states were entitled to enrol and vote in Commonwealth elections, and 1962 before this was extended to all Indigenous Australians.

A few Aboriginal people participated in the official celebrations to mark Federation. They stood to form part of an arch for the street procession in Brisbane (Qld). Their participation was at odds with the fact that the new Commonwealth had powers to make laws for all Australians except Aboriginal people. The states retained this right. Indigenous Australians were not even to be counted in the census of Australian residents held initially every ten years then every five years.

At the turn of the century, it was widely believed that Aboriginal people were dying out. Most lived in poverty on the outskirts of country towns or cities, or they were isolated from the rest of society on missions and reserves. They had been forced into a dependency on government handouts. Some worked on pastoral stations but were often only paid in kind. The number of Aboriginal people of mixed descent increased as white settlement expanded. Early in the century, governments began to remove children of mixed descent from their mothers and their communities in an attempt to make them 'white'. They placed them in welfare institutions and homes or on missions.

Non-British settlers

Not all arrivals in the 19th century were from Britain and Ireland. By 1901 settlers from countries on the European continent and Asia made up two per cent of the population. Most Europeans arrived in numbers too small to establish or maintain distinctive communities in the long term. They intermarried and had Australian-born children. Their presence was accepted and they were not seen as a threat to the dominant Anglo-Celtic culture.

The largest group of European settlers were Germans.

These children pictured in April 1900 at New Mecklenburg school in South Australia's Barossa Valley lived in an area closely settled by their German forebears. The first arrivals in the late 1830s had fled from religious persecution in their homeland. Later arrivals had heard that opportunities to make a better life existed in the colony. Germans had also settled in the eastern colonies, in groups and as individuals and families.

Except for those Germans who had stayed in close-knit rural communities, large group settlement among European settlers in the 19th century was not common. Generally most Europeans arrived in Australia as young, single men seeking work and their fortune in the rapidly expanding colonies, especially in the gold rush era of the 1850s and the boom years of the 1880s. Some were seamen who had deserted their ships.

They settled across the continent. They were highly mobile and worked in the cities and in the country in a wide variety of trades and businesses, but especially as unskilled labourers.

F Jensen who owned a jewellery business in Gympie (Qld) in the 1870s was one of many Scandinavians who settled in Australia. From the 1870s, the Queensland government offered assisted passages and land grants to Swedes, Norwegians and Danes as well as Finns, recruiting them especially as unskilled rural workers, in particular as cane cutters in the sugar industry.

The Joubert family were prominent French land owners, merchants and civic leaders in Hunters Hill (NSW) when this portrait was taken of Numa Joubert and his wife Margaret in c1890. Numa arrived as a baby in Sydney in 1841, with his parents Didier and Lise Joubert, and his uncle Jules. From the late 1840s Didier and Jules began to buy land along the waterfront at Hunters Hill. They built fine houses and operated a ferry service to Sydney. Jules and Didier were early mayors of the Hunters Hill district. The reputation and activities of the Joubert brothers attracted other French settlers to the district.

Other European arrivals in the 19th century included Italians, Greeks, Poles, Maltese and Russians, including those of Jewish background. Many French settlers worked in the emerging wine industry. Small numbers of Channel Islanders with their Norman-French background had also settled in the colonies. Americans and Canadians had also arrived in small numbers.

'The Yellow Peril'

Many Australians felt threatened by the presence of Chinese settlers who had begun to arrive in Australia with the 1850s gold rushes. They came mostly from southern China where by 1842 Britain had forced China to open up its ports to foreign trade and control. From the 1860s 'Afghans', Indians and Pacific Islanders were specifically recruited to work in northern and outback Australia.

The participation of Melbourne's Chinese residents in the celebrations to mark the opening of the first Federal parliament on 9 May by the Duke of York, suggested that they were, at another level, an active and at least tolerated, group in the wider community.

Chinese were the largest group of Asian settlers in Australia. Although many returned to China after the gold rushes, some stayed and by 1901 there were 30,000 Chinese in the major cities and across Australia. They worked as labourers, market gardeners, shopkeepers, laundry operators, cooks and shearers. They were merchants and businessmen. Chinese also worked in the sugar and banana industries in Queensland.

Most settlers from non-European countries had come to Australia because of connections within the British Empire. Some were British subjects from other parts of the Empire.

They were overwhelmingly young, single men.

'Afghans' had been recruited largely from the northern part of the Indian subcontinent, and also from Iran, Egypt and Turkey, to operate camel trains to carry supplies throughout outback Australia. They were all, regardless of place of origin, loosely referred to as 'Afghans' by colonial authorities because of their similar appearance and dress and the common bond of their Islamic faith. These camel drivers were pictured at Cunnamulla in Queensland at the turn of the century.

Around 4000 Indians from British India and Ceylon (now Sri Lanka) worked in the sugar and banana industries in northern New South Wales and Queensland. With worldwide population shifts common in the 19th century, Indians also moved to other parts of the British Empire, including South Africa, Kenya, Fiji, Malaya and Singapore.

Six thousand Pacific Islanders, also known as Kanakas, were working on contracts as indentured labourers in the Queensland sugar industry at the time of Federation. Most came from British-controlled south sea islands. Although this photograph shows men working the fields, small numbers of Pacific Islander women also worked on Queensland's cane plantations.

Owners of cane fields and sugar mills argued that non-white workers were best suited to labouring work in tropical areas. From the 1860s, agents for the Queensland colonial government recruited 62,000 Pacific Islanders, mostly men and by force. Treatment had frequently been harsh and mortality rates were high, especially in the 1870s. The use of Pacific Islanders on plantations was controversial, attracting criticism for being a form of slave labour which had no place in Australia, the 'workingman's paradise'.

Another British Empire connection led to the recruitment of Japanese to work in Australia.

This late 19th century photograph shows Japanese workers sorting pearl shell at Broome (WA). In 1894 Britain and Japan signed the Anglo-Japanese Commercial Treaty. Under its arrangements, the Queensland government recruited restricted numbers of Japanese for plantation work and the pearling industry based on Thursday Island. In 1901, three and a half thousand Japanese worked in the pearling industry on Thursday Island (Qld) and in Broome. Malays and Filipinos worked there too, especially as boat crew.

From the 1880s Lebanese settlers began to arrive in Australia. They came with Turkish papers, Lebanon being a part of the Turkish Empire until 1919. Most were Christians with an affinity for Western culture and were unhappy with Turkish Muslim rule over their land. Economic factors also played a role in their departure.

Most Lebanese settlers became hawkers in Australia, selling their wares in pastoral and farming areas. By the time of Federation, many had become shopkeepers, especially in the drapery and haberdashery trade, in country towns and major cities. For Lebanese settlers, such as the Khyat family who owned a store in Melbourne, shop ownership was a sign of increased prosperity and the arrival of wives and children a sign of permanent settlement in Australia.

In 1901 the Asian pearling workers in Broome (WA) participated in a procession to celebrate the proclamation of Federation. Their float was aptly named HMS *Commonwealth*. Ironically, they were celebrating the launch of a new ship of state, the Commonwealth of Australia, which did not want non-European 'crewmen' on board.

No Entry

Since the 1850s, colonial governments had restricted the entry of Chinese into Australia. By the end of the century, they had turned their attention to all non-Europeans. Emerging trade unions feared that cheap 'foreign' labour would undermine hard-won wage levels and conditions. Factory owners feared competition in certain urban industries, such as furniture-making. Restrictions, however, were not uniform across the colonies.

By the turn of the century, a belief in the superiority of white people and notions of racial purity had become popular in Australian society.

A strong argument for Federation was that national legislation, binding on all the states, was the only way to keep Australia white.

1900s – 1910s

ONE PEOPLE

In May 1901 the new Federal Parliament settled down to the business of governing the nation. This Parliament and subsequent governments began to establish policies on populating, developing and defending the nation, all of which were designed to keep Australia white.

... WE SHOULD BE ONE PEOPLE, AND REMAIN ONE PEOPLE, WITHOUT THE ADMIXTURE OF OTHER RACES.

Alfred Deakin, Attorney-General in the first Federal Parliament opened on 9 May 1901 by the Duke of York in its temporary location in Melbourne's Exhibition Buildings.

Populate or Perish

Both the national and state governments wanted to fill Australia's vast empty spaces to keep Australia secure from threat and to create economic strength through rural export industries. Immigrants were seen as key to the success of this plan.

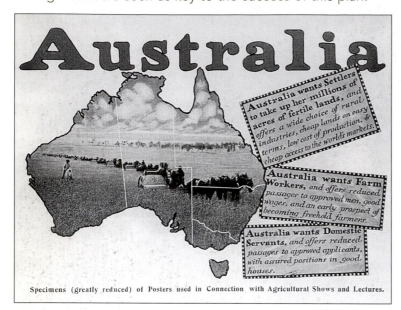

Specimens (greatly reduced) of Posters used in Connection with Agricultural Shows and Lectures.

After Federation the states retained the right to conduct their own immigration assistance schemes, as they had done as colonies in the 19th century. Immigration policy and practice became part of the complex web of federal and state relations after 1901. In 1906 the Commonwealth agreed to fund advertising campaigns to attract British settlers and in 1913 began to subsidise the states' assisted passage programs.

'Blood of Empire'

The focus was on attracting settlers from the British Isles, single men and women and families.

Immigrants who landed in Australian ports, such as Fremantle (shown), were mostly English, especially from London and southern England. The remainder were from Scotland, Wales and from Ireland. They were part of a huge movement of people leaving Europe for opportunities in the 'New World', including the United States of America, Canada, Australia, Africa and South America. This movement had begun in the 19th century.

The Paterson and Adams families left Scotland on the White Star liner *Suevie*, arriving in Fremantle in 1910 to settle in Western Australia. They were among nearly 200 000 immigrants who set sail with high hopes from Britain for Australia between 1907 and 1914, with the peak of arrivals in 1912. About half came on assisted passages.

These new British settlers merged into an Anglo-Celtic society formed by previous generations of mainly British immigrants. They brought with them, though, the cultural practices and attitudes current in Britain at the time of their departure.

Settlers stepped onto a continent that had been occupied for at least 40 000 years by Indigenous peoples. By the turn of the 20th century, colonists to Australia had dispossessed them of the traditional lands that had always sustained them socially, spiritually and economically.

The group photograph: group recruitment, arrival and settlement

Top: The Immigration League of Australasia, established in 1905, was one of the non-government agencies that promoted immigration to Australia in Britain. It also aimed to educate Australians on the need for an increased rural population and gave practical advice and assistance to new arrivals. This group of British ex-servicemen, some of whom had served in India, and other army reservists, was assisted to Australia by the British Immigration League. They were welcomed at the League's receiving depot in Glebe, Sydney in July 1913.

Above: These 'farm workers for New South Wales' were typical of the single men and women, mostly from the working classes, who responded to the call for unskilled rural labourers and domestic servants and arrived in Australia in large groups. To qualify for assisted passage, men had to be under forty-five and women under thirty-five.

Emigration from Ireland was particularly strong in the second half of the 19th century in the wake of the Great Famine, but as Ireland slowly recovered, Irish arrivals declined in the early years of the 20th century.

These girls, recruited in Ireland and England, were pictured outside their hostel after arrival in Adelaide in 1913. They typified those who did come. They were young, single women destined for domestic service.

The federal and state governments wanted immigrants to settle on the land. Mr J C Gomme, who arrived from the Isle of Wight in 1905, was one of many English land settlers who took up farming blocks in the south-west of Western Australia. The Western Australian government cleared the land, surveyed townships and built roads and railways. Farming blocks adjoined each other, creating group settlements that were intended to compensate new settlers for the isolation and distance from the capital city, Perth.

These British settlers in the Tamar Valley
orchard district in Tasmania were labelled as
'Empire Settlers' when their photograph
appeared in the *Weekly Courier* in 1913.

In the early 20th century, British emigrants
were heading to lands of the Empire, rather
than to the United States of America.
Destinations included Australia, South Africa
and New Zealand. The British and Australian
governments were pleased by the notion of
the 'blood of Empire' flowing out from Britain
to its far-flung colonies and dominions.

The myth and the reality

A New South Wales Department of Agriculture photograph in 1910 showed new arrivals loading chaff on Brunskills Station at Wagga Wagga. Such farmers and farm workers fulfilled the government's expectation that immigrants would 'take up Australia's millions of acres of fertile lands'.

But most immigrants had come from urban areas in Britain. They ended up finding unskilled work in the factories and foundries of major cities and living nearby in workers' cottages, as had Australian-born workers. Tradesmen, such as carpenters and bricklayers, readily found work in the building industry.

Leaving Europe

Just as they had in the 19th century, small numbers of immigrants from the European continent arrived in Australia in the early years of the 20th century.

They were mostly young, single men. They moved around Australia, finding unskilled work in mines, smelters and quarries. They worked on the wharves, on farms and in factories. They cleared land, cut timber and joined cane gangs. They were employed in railway, road and dam construction.

They faced exploitation by some employers and the distrust of Australia's emerging trade unions. But with plenty of work and good wages, they stayed on, gaining reputations as reliable workers.

Others opened shops and restaurants, factories and businesses. They became farmers and market gardeners. Some arrived with trade and professional skills and worked as land surveyors, engineers, musicians and teachers.

With unemployment and overpopulation of the British island colony of Malta, emigration was encouraged, especially to other parts of the Empire. Between 1911 and 1919 two thousand arrived in Australia. They were not included in assisted passage schemes, due largely to concerns about their impact on the Australian workforce.

Maltese arrivals found work at the Mt Lyell copper mines in Tasmania, a major employer of immigrant labour. These men were pictured in the road gang in 1913. Working conditions were tough. Many moved on, working in railway construction in New South Wales and the Northern Territory and on the canefields.

Between 1910 and 1920 Greek settlers Mick and John Kanis had a fruit stall in Perth (WA). This photograph was taken at the end of World War I (1914-1918). They had decorated their stall with patriotic Australian flags and bunting, perhaps in order to keep up their trade, as the neighbouring stall encouraged customers to 'patronise a returned soldier'.

Below: There were only a few hundred Bulgarians in Australia early in the 20th century. How had they heard of opportunities in distant Australia? Many found unskilled work in the new Broken Hill (NSW) mines. This group was photographed there in 1917. They dressed formally.

They posed with straight backs and an air of pride in keeping with their place in history as pioneers. At the centre of their story, as if to embody all their dreams and hopes for the future, the men placed a little boy, James Vassel Staiff who was one of the first of the new Australian-born generation.

A record party of over two hundred German immigrants, from the provinces of Rheinland and Westphalen, arrived in Brisbane in June 1910. The *Brisbane Courier* remarked that they all appeared to be 'a fine stamp of colonist. The men are for the most part typical German farmers, and peasants of the better class, hardy and well built…'. They had been nominated by Lutheran minister, Rev Niemeyer, of Hatton Vale (Qld) who 'has been instrumental in bringing many hundreds of colonists from the Fatherland'. They were planning to settle in the Gayndah district.

By the early part of the 20th century, most German Australians were Australian-born. Large-scale arrivals had virtually stopped by the 1880s. The arrival of German settlers in 1910 was unusual. They were probably among the last Germans to come to Australia before Germany and Britain went to war in 1914.

By 1914 there were 10 000 Italian settlers across Australia. Italians from Molfetta brought their fishing knowledge and skills to the ports of Fremantle, Port Adelaide, Port Pirie and Sydney. There they established close-knit communities, joined over the years by family members and neighbours from Molfetta, in a process known as chain migration.

Many Italian settlers established small businesses in the large cities. Carlo De Angelis, pictured by his horse and buggy in 1911, employed other Italians in his grocery business in Prahran, a Melbourne suburb.

By 1911 there were four and a half thousand Russian settlers in Australia. Some were left-wing political exiles, escaping the Tsarist regime and often became involved in Australian trade unions. Many Russians headed to Queensland after arrival. Mr and Mrs Kreanoff were photographed as they came off the ship in Brisbane in January 1912. They were intending to farm at Mackay.

Jewish settlers came from Britain and Western and Eastern Europe. J L Komersarook arrived from Russia in 1914, first working as a hawker. From two suitcases he sold ladies' wear. In 1915 he opened a store in Ballarat. He returned to Russia in 1920 to bring his family to Australia.

20th century Jewish arrivals joined thriving communities, especially in Sydney and Melbourne. Most earlier arrivals had come from Britain. They identified with English culture and were strongly represented in Australian social, civic, political, business and professional life. The arrival of Jews from the European continent led to some initial tension with English Jews. In 1913 a group of Eastern European Jews established a farming settlement at Shepparton in Victoria.

Keeping Australia white

In 1901 the first Federal parliament passed the *Immigration Restriction Act* to ban the entry of non-European people.

This Act was part of the White Australia Policy, although its regulations could also be used to prevent the entry of white immigrants considered by immigration authorities to be 'undesirable' because of criminal records, mental condition or political views.

Anyone with a non-European background wanting to enter Australia had to sit for a dictation test of 50 words in a European language (amended in 1905 to 'any prescribed language'). Customs officers were instructed to choose the appropriate test to ensure failure. Failure meant exclusion.

Although the Act was amended over the years, usually to cover loopholes, its purpose never changed.

The dictation test was based on a system used in Natal Province, South Africa. It caused much debate in parliament. Some disliked the idea of using an indirect method to ban unwanted immigrants. But the merit of the dictation test was that it purported to exclude on the basis of education rather than race and was a concession to the British government uneasy about one part of its Empire offending other British subjects by prohibiting entry on the grounds of race.

It's not as if the non-European population in Australia accepted their fate without question. William Ah Ket, a Melbourne barrister and the only Chinese lawyer for some years, was one face of Chinese opposition to the many laws which discriminated against them. Merchants and Chinese associations, including the Chinese Chamber of Commerce also tried, although in no united way, to change Australia's position on non-Europeans arrivals and settlers. The protests made little impact.

The dictation test was a successful method of exclusion, especially when combined with heavy penalties imposed on shipping lines for bringing in prohibited immigrants.

Ships' captains were required to photograph and thumbprint non-European crew members. This information was then used on posters to track them down if they absconded. Usually the government offered a reward for information leading to their arrest and deportation. Most eluded authorities. Although all the sailors on this poster were Chinese, other non-European deserters included Indian sailors from Fiji and India. Prominent members of the Chinese community feared that illegal arrivals would adversely affect the standing of Chinese residents in the wider society.

The non-European population in Australia declined dramatically after 1901, although the *Immigration Restriction Act* did not totally prohibit their entry. Merchants, students and tourists from Japan, India and China could gain entry with temporary permits if they had passports from their own countries. Unskilled labourers, most likely to threaten Australian working standards, were not exempted entrants. However, Japanese pearl divers and Malay and Filipino boat crew were allowed in on temporary permits and were exempt from the dictation test.

Form No. 21.   COMMONWEALTH OF AUSTRALIA.   No. 477

Immigration Restriction Acts 1901-1905 and Regulations.

CERTIFICATE EXEMPTING FROM DICTATION TEST.

I, *John Baxter* *Actg* the Collector of Customs
for the State of *New South Wales* in the said Commonwealth
hereby certify that *Go Gee (Wife of Hu Gee)*
hereinafter described, who is leaving the Commonwealth temporarily, will be exempted
from the provisions of paragraph (a) of Section 3 of the Act if he returns to the Commonwealth within a period of *three years* from this date.

Date *Augst 08*   *Baxter*
Actg Collector of Customs

DESCRIPTION.

Nationality *Chinese*	Birthplace *Canton*
Age *26 years*	Complexion *Dark*
Height —	Hair *Dark*
Build *Medium*	Eyes *Brown*
Particular marks —	

(For impression of hand see back of this document.)

PHOTOGRAPHS.

Full Face :—   Profile :—

Date of departure *Augst 08.*   Destination *China*
Ship *Empire*
Date of return *5.6.15*   Ship *Easter*
Port *Sydney*

W. Donohoe
Customs Officer

F. Bragg

COMPARED WITH DUPLICATE AND FOUND TO AGREE

By Authority : ROBT. S. BRAIN, Government Printer, Melbourne.

Living in white Australia

The 1901 *Immigration Restriction Act* and the 1903
Naturalisation Act adversely affected non-European residents.

Wives and children were barred from joining
husbands in Australia after 1903, but
discretionary exemptions, usually for six
months, allowed them to enter, especially if
they were related to prominent members of
the Chinese community of long-standing
in Australia.

Here Horsham (Vic) resident, Poon Gooey,
posed for an identification photograph before
a trip to China in 1910. In 1911 his wife joined
him initially for six months, although this was
extended while she awaited the births of two
children. In 1913, despite wider community
support for her to remain in Australia, the
government insisted on her departure. Poon
Gooey and her children went with her.

About 47 000 non-European residents,
30 000 of whom were Chinese, were living in
Australia when the *Immigration Restriction
Act* was passed. Later census records
showed a declining population, a clear
indication of the success of the Act.
Lebanese settlers protested at being initially
classified as non-European, emphasising
their affinity with Western culture.
Discretionary exemptions were granted and
by the mid 1920s the Act no longer applied
to Lebanese arrivals. Exemptions for Indian
wives and children were also introduced.

Opposite: Non-European residents were
allowed to return to Australia after a visit to
their homeland for family or business reasons
without having to sit for a dictation test.
Before departure from Australia, they had to
apply and pay for an exemption certificate
which included a photograph for
identification.

The story of the Tong Way family

The Tong Way family, pictured here in Ballarat at the turn of the century, reveals the impact of White Australia on Chinese and other non-European residents. They were members of a community that was forced to change but still survived despite the restrictions they faced.

All members of the family wore Western dress and used Christian names. This was common in Chinese families by the early 20th century.

Without new young arrivals from China, John Tong Way became part of the ageing Chinese and non-European male population.

John was a Presbyterian minister. Conversion to Christianity accelerated the assimilation of non-European residents in the wider community and helped to counter the negative stereotype of Chinese as gamblers and opium addicts. The Christian churches protested against Australia's racist laws and attitudes.

Joseph Tong Way, aged 10 when he arrived in Australia in 1893, was not naturalised, when, under the *Naturalisation Act* of 1903, non-European residents born overseas could no longer take out citizenship. They could not vote or draw the aged pension. Joseph remained a resident 'alien' till his death in 1956.

Before World War I, Joseph returned briefly to China to work. He was like many non-European men who spent periods of time working in their countries of origin or visiting families. The *Immigration Restriction Act* allowed them to return to Australia, exempt from the dictation test, if they could prove previous residency.

Joseph chose to marry a European woman, rather than return to China for a marriage partner. After 1901, intermarriage became more common, resulting in changes in traditional cultural practice in Australia.

Mary Tong Way was one of just a few non-European women in Australia. Generally Chinese and Indian men left their wives and families back in China and India. After 1903, it was Australian entry restrictions rather than cultural practice that prevented families from joining husbands in Australia. This also encouraged men to return to their homeland.

Samuel, Doris and Hedley were part of the Australian-born generations who moved into the professions, business and land ownership. The Tong Way children went to Australian schools, a change from past practice when Chinese children went back to China for their education. Chinese schools were uncommon in Australia due to a lack of teachers. Samuel and Doris became teachers and Hedley a public servant. In the 20th century few young Chinese in Australia had been born in China.

Under pressure from anti-Chinese leagues and Australian workers and businesses, most state governments also passed legislation against non-European residents. For instance, in 1904 the Western Australian government passed the *Factories Act*, placing restrictions on Chinese ownership and operation of factories and businesses, in particular on furniture factories and Chinese laundries such as Soon Lee's, pictured in Perth in the early 1900s. The states also passed legislation that included various restrictions on land ownership, mining activities, canecutting, and entry to the public service. Trade unions excluded non-European workers. Chinese worked as hawkers, fruit-pickers and market gardeners, in jobs which did not compete directly with Australians.

Prejudice often surfaced at the community level in White Australia. When Daniel Poon Num, banana merchant and restaurateur, attempted to purchase a house in the Adelaide suburb of Rose Park in 1913, neighbours petitioned against it. He won out, however, and he and his family lived there until 1915 when hard times forced the family to move.

Deportation

In 1901 Federal Parliament passed the *Pacific Islands Labourers Act* to ban the use of Pacific Islanders as contract labourers in the Queensland sugar industry and to deport those already in Australia.

The sight of Pacific Islanders hoeing Queensland's cane fields on large plantations had been a familiar sight since the 1860s. But when this photograph was taken at Herbert River in 1902, the use of indentured labour from the south sea islands was soon to end.

The use of their labour was banned after March 1904, with only a limited number of licences to import labourers issued in 1902 and 1903.

Despite sugar industry concerns of collapse without cheap indentured labourers, Federal Parliament was determined to eliminate non-white workers from the Australian work force. To compensate cane growers, parliament introduced tariffs on foreign sugar. Until 1913 a bounty was paid to growers who used only white labour, a situation which affected Indian canecutters, as well as Pacific Islanders. The nature of sugar production changed too, with new technology and smaller cane farms replacing plantations.

This group of Pacific Islanders mustered at Cairns courthouse in November 1906 were the first of nearly 4000 deported under the Act and returned to the islands. Return was traumatic for many. They had become strangers in their villages after years in Australia on repeated contracts. In some instances, authorities failed to return them to their correct home island. They abandoned them on other islands, putting their lives in peril from hostile villagers, unwilling to accept them in their midst.

Other photographs, however, record the ongoing presence of Pacific Islanders in Queensland despite the deportation order. An unnamed family near Mackay in 1908 was among the 1600 or so granted permission to stay in Australia. Exemptions were extended to the aged and frail, to those who had been in Australia for a long time, married couples with Australian-born children and to those who owned or leased land.

Who was to replace the Pacific Islanders?

Once it was conceded in the 1890s by the sugar industry that island labour would be phased out in a federated Australia, Australian-born, British, German, Scandinavian and Indian workers began to be employed as canecutters.

This gang working in the canefields near Ingham (Qld) in 1911 were Finns.

THE CHANGING FACE OF AUSTRALIA

Southern European settlers, including Italians, Greeks, Croatians, Maltese, Spaniards and Basques, were also readily employed because of their reputation for working hard over long hours. They were often treated by growers as substitute 'white' indentured labourers. This led to conflict with trade unions fearing that cheap 'foreign' labour would erode Australian workers' conditions.

In 1907 Spanish workers, mostly from Catalonia, were recruited by the Colonial Sugar Refining Company.

Those photographed were typical of the Southern European recruits. Young, single men, leaving behind family poverty, unemployment, social change, and political strife. They had few skills, little education or English, just a dream that hard work would bring prosperity in the New World.

Not all cane gang workers arrived in large organised groups. Some had deserted ship in Australian ports. Some arrived on their own. Others came with brothers, cousins and village neighbours. Once in Australia, word was that a few years of gruelling, but well-paid work in a cane gang in northern Australia meant the opportunity to buy a farm of one's own, especially with smaller farms replacing plantations.

A snapshot of Australia

Photographs taken in the early decades of the 20th century, though often formally posed, reveal a vibrant and diverse Australian cultural life.

On 1 January 1901 Kalgoorlie (WA) residents crowded along the streets to watch the Commonwealth Day procession. Like other Australians, they were celebrating a new united nation. But within that new nation was a diversity of allegiances, cultural practices and interests.

Opposite: delegates to the Hibernian Society Conference at Geraldton (Qld) in 1906 posed in front of symbols of Ireland, the shamrock and the Celtic cross. Irish settlers were a significant group amongst Anglo-Celtic Australians. Their Catholic faith, with its close-knit parish life and their objection to English control over their island country, set them apart. Not all Irish settlers were Catholic, though, and a photograph of an Irish Protestant Loyal Orange Lodge meeting would have suggested a different set of Irish allegiances.

In 1915 the Beverley Cricket Club played that most English of sporting games at Western Australia's Country Cricket Week and a team from St Finbar's Catholic parish won the Queensland Irish Association's hurling competition. Cricket thrived in Australia's English-based sporting life, whereas it was harder to sustain interest in hurling, a distinctive Irish game, beyond the Irish-born generation who brought the skills of the game with them to Australia.

Photographs of English regional groupings, such as this gathering of the Northumberland and Durham Association in Gympie (Qld) in 1916, are harder to find after World War I. Regional ties generally faded with the Australian-born generation sitting in the front row. Such photographs are also a reminder that English immigrants brought a diversity of dialects, cultural practices and memories with them that also faded as the young ones adopted Australian-based loyalties and traditions.

Descendants of early Polish settlers attended a Polish school at Polish Hill River in South Australia in 1915. Language and religion are key to the continuation of cultural practice in a new land. In 1925 the Polish school closed due to a lack of pupils, a far cry from the 1870s when the school first opened to teach the children of local Polish settlers.

Members of Brisbane's Greek community flew the Greek flag at a picnic at 18 Mile Rocks in 1911. Many settlers maintained links with their homeland and closely followed its fortunes and crises. A year later Greece was part of an uneasy Balkans alliance fighting for independence against the Turkish Ottoman Empire.

念紀遊河旦元部支黨民國扶普澳西年八拾國民華

Many Chinese maintained an active interest in the political reform movement in China. At Point Walter in Western Australia members of the Chinese Nationalist Party made a stand about events back in their homeland, whilst enjoying a boating picnic. Chinese around Australia celebrated the birth of the Chinese Republic in 1911 with picnics and fireworks.

THE CHANGING FACE OF AUSTRALIA

Western Australian Aborigines met for a 'corroboree' in 1909 and in 1912 at Killalpaninna Lutheran Mission in South Australia candidates for baptism came together for a group photograph.

The white dress of this German Lutheran bride who married in South Australia in the early years of the 20th century marked a break away from the traditions of her mother and grandmother who wore black or dark-coloured dresses on their wedding day. Even the close-knit German communities over time adopted some of the cultural practices of their predominantly Anglo-Celtic neighbours.

Under Union Jacks, the Australian flag and the flags of their countries, members of Queensland's Scandinavian communities enjoyed a masquerade ball in the South Brisbane Town Hall in 1906. Gathering for social occasions was a welcome break from the pressures and difficulties that many immigrants faced.

A group of Italian settlers from the Aeolian Islands posed at the first annual picnic for Melbourne fruiterers in 1906 at Sorrento, a seaside town on Port Philip Bay. It was their occupation as fruiterers that brought them to this picnic and united them with others there. The presence of women and children was also a reminder that marriage and family ties were key to their separate and continuing identity as Italians.

When this photograph was published in a Queensland newspaper in 1911 it was entitled *The Immigrants First Christmas in Queensland*. It is a heart-rending example of how immigrants faced the shock of the new. These immigrants celebrated Christmas in a new way in a new land.

1914 - 1918
AUSTRALIANS AT WAR

After decades of forming opposing alliances and strengthening their armed forces and naval fleets, Britain, Germany and their allies went to war against each other in 1914.

As a member of Britain's Empire, Australia sent an Australian Imperial Force, the AIF, to the battlefields of Gallipoli in Turkey, Palestine in the Middle-East, and France and Belgium in Europe.

The war, known then as the Great War and later as World War I, lasted from August 1914 until November 1918. During this time, immigration virtually stopped as passenger shipping declined. Although the battlefields were on distant shores, the war touched the lives of most Australians. Men became soldiers, or worked in ship construction and the production of foodstuffs. Women watched their menfolk march off to war and then mourned their loss. They volunteered as nurses or worked in factories. They joined the Red Cross, sold badges for the war effort, and assembled comfort parcels for troops overseas. Their children helped them.

For their Empire Day celebrations in May 1915, just a month after Australian soldiers landed on Gallipoli's shores, the children at Princes Hill State School in the Melbourne suburb of Carlton (Vic) lined up with their Union Jacks, in a display of loyalty repeated across the Australian continent. Only a small number of Australians, with pacifist or socialist convictions, publicly opposed the war.

'To many young Australians Great Britain was a fabled country, of which they had learned at their mother's knee, the home of wonderful things – of the many stories of childhood, of snow and lawns and rivers and castles and wonders seen only on Christmas cards. In the common language the motherland was still often spoken of as "home".' *CEW Bean*

Anzac Day

By the end of the war Empire Day celebrations had been joined by a ceremony which was Australia's own. On 25 April 1916, in what was to become an annual event, Australians remembered their fallen soldiers. In the early 1920s many Australian towns and suburbs erected memorials to the fallen. The dogged bravery and achievements of soldiers of the AIF had boosted Australia's sense of national pride and confidence. Australians began to see their country as a nation in its own right.

The soldiers who marched to war

The majority of volunteers who marched off to training camps and sailed overseas were Australian-born. They went off to defend the 'Mother Country', the home of their parents and grandparents, the pioneering immigrants of the 19th century.

About a third of the early enlistments, such as this group marching off to training camp in Melbourne in 1914, were young settlers who had immigrated to Australia from Britain in the first decade of the 20th century. They found themselves in uniform, sailing back to the 'Old World'. Others returned to Britain to join regiments affiliated with their place of origin or family or to which they belonged as reservists.

Among British-Australians, Scots enlisted proportionately in greater numbers and were significant in the officer ranks. Major General Sir William Bridges who died of wounds received at Gallipoli in May 1915 and Sir Thomas Glasgow and Sir James McCoy, both commanders of AIF divisions, were Scots.

Recruits with Danish, Polish, French, Jewish and other European backgrounds also joined the Australian Imperial Force (AIF).

Australian Jews were in all ranks but the best-known was John Monash, a civil engineer from Melbourne, shown here marching in an Anzac Day parade in 1935. As Lieutenant-General, he became Commander-in-Chief of the Australia Corps in France in 1918. There he played a significant role in setting the strategies for the final battles of the war.

Danish settlers joined the AIF because Germany had long been an aggressor along its common border with Denmark and had annexed the Danish territories of Schleswig and Holstein in the 1860s. Some French settlers returned to France to join the French army.

Soldiers of Irish birth or parentage enlisted too. The war was a time of conflicting loyalties for many Irish-born Australians, especially after the uprising by Sinn Fein, Irish independence fighters, was brutally quelled in Dublin in Easter 1916 by British troops. Archbishop Mannix, the Irish-born Catholic archbishop of Melbourne, was an outspoken opponent of the Australian government's attempts to introduce conscription in 1916 and 1917, although the defeat of the proposal rested on more factors than the Irish Catholic vote alone.

Fighting other battles

Aboriginal Australians were not counted as citizens, yet around four hundred enlisted for service. A number died in battle.

Chinese Australians faced their own battles in Australia against racism and discrimination. Despite this, some volunteered for duty.

Hedley Tong Way and his brother Samuel enlisted in the AIF. Samuel had tried twice before 1916 to join but was rejected because he was non-European, although he had been born in Australia and was an Australian citizen. At the end of 1916, after China had entered the war on the Allies' side, both brothers were accepted and served in the Signal Corps in France. As did so many others, Hedley posed for a formal photograph in his uniform before his departure for overseas duty. His sister, Doris, stood beside him. Both men survived the war and returned home.

'The enemy within the gates'

Australian residents who were citizens of Germany, the Austro-Hungarian Empire, Bulgaria and Turkey were declared 'enemy aliens'. They faced internment, police surveillance, dismissal from employment and restrictions in their daily lives for the duration of the war. They endured the suspicions and antagonism of neighbours and damage to their property. At the same time, their Australian-born relatives volunteered for duty overseas to fight the German enemy.

There were about 33 000 German 'enemy aliens' in Australia at the outbreak of war, with major areas of German rural settlement in the Barossa Valley and the Adelaide Hills in South Australia, in Victoria and in Queensland. There were another three thousand Austro-Hungarians. Most of these were Dalmatian Croats who worked on the Western Australian goldfields. The number of Bulgarian and Turkish citizens in Australia was small.

There was an initial rush of applications for naturalisation when war began. But even this declaration of commitment to Australia and the British Empire did not protect German residents from anti-German hysteria, and in some cases, internment. Thousands of other Australian-born citizens with German parentage were also targets of suspicion and aggression.

Internment camps operated in all states. The largest camp was at Liverpool (NSW), shown here with internees using gymnastic equipment.

Some German nationals voluntarily submitted to internment after they were dismissed from their jobs and had no means of support. Others had encountered aggressive behaviour and requested internment for their own safety.

About 7000 'enemy aliens' were interned, although many of these were later released under police surveillance. This number included a thousand German nationals brought to Australia, at Britain's request, from the Pacific Islands and Ceylon. At the end of the war a thousand internees still remained in internment camps.

Conditions in the camps were basic. But they were particularly harsh on Torrens Island (SA), a sandy island in the midst of mangrove swamps. It was a makeshift camp built mostly of tents.

Berrima internment camp in New South Wales held mostly ships' officers and Trial Bay, also in New South Wales, was for well-educated single men. In 1915 camps at Enogerra in Queensland and on Torrens Island in South Australia were closed and internees transferred to Liverpool. A hundred and fifty women and children, left without any means of support when the family breadwinner was interned, were accommodated at Bourke (NSW) and later at a new camp near the Molonglo River (ACT).

Toilet facilities were primitive on Torrens Island. Internees dug new holes each day and covered the old ones with sand. Internees reported incidences of beatings and cruel treatment by guards to military authorities who investigated the complaints but offered no compensation. The major complaint from many internees, however, was the injustice of their internment in the first place.

'I was born in Germany in 1856, came to Australia in October 1876 and was naturalised in 1911. I am married to an Australian born woman of English parentage. I am a farmer and own land in South Australia. I was arrested on the 28th April 1915 and taken to Keswick and later to Torrens Island. For four nights I was left without any blankets, and had to sleep in a tent on the bare ground. The sanitary accommodation and the life itself at Torrens Island was horrible.'
Statutory declaration by internee, Liverpool camp, 1917

Internees found ways to alleviate the boredom and frustration of enforced inactivity. They formed choirs and music bands. They produced newspapers and put on theatrical performances. On Torrens Island in 1915 they dressed up as court ladies and jester for the German Kaiser's birthday.

In a twist of fate, some Australians of German background were interned in Germany during the war. German settlers in Australia had long maintained close connections with their homeland. German publishing firms supplied religious books for the various Lutheran congregations and those wishing to become Lutheran pastors often studied at seminaries in Germany. At the outbreak of war these six young Australians were studying at Neuendettelsau Lutheran seminary in Bavaria, Germany and were interned along with British civilians at Ruhleben camp in Berlin, where they were photographed. After two and a half years they were released to do farm work and were also permitted to continue their studies. After the war, they completed further studies in the United States before returning home to Australia.

Five thousand German nationals were deported or voluntarily repatriated between May 1919 and June 1920 on nine specially designated ships. In 1920, two years after the end of the war, the *Immigration Act* was amended, banning the entry of Germans, Austrians, Bulgarians, Hungarians and Turks for five years, although the ban on Turks was not lifted until 1930.

In 1917 Hahndorf, a township established in 1839 by German settlers in the Adelaide Hills, was renamed Ambleside. In South Australia alone forty-two place names and others in Queensland and Victoria, were changed in an attempt to obliterate the evidence of German settlements in Australia. Only a few townships reverted to their original names in the years after the war.

Under the *War Precautions Act*, German settlers faced fines or imprisonment for failure to comply with a barrage of regulations, mostly to do with registering as an 'enemy alien'. German residents were not allowed to own firearms, carrier pigeons, telephones or cameras. Any shares they owned had to be transferred to the Public Trustee for the duration of the war. They were not allowed to purchase or lease property or operate mines. But numerous exemptions to these regulations were granted.

The war had a devastating impact on the use of the German language, especially in Lutheran churches and schools. In South Australia, fifty-two Lutheran schools were taken over by the Education Department and English became the language of instruction. In Victoria schools were also required to teach in English. In New South Wales and Queensland Lutheran schools were closed.

In 1912 the members of the Deutscher Klub in Brisbane were photographed relaxing in their clubrooms. With the declaration of war, all German clubs and associations were closed, many never to reopen. German language newspapers and other publications were banned until 1925. Aboriginal missions run by German missionaries in outback Australia struggled to survive.

Before the war Germans had been known as hardworking, honest settlers and good neighbours. With war, they became 'the German menace'. German Australians were denounced for spying and other supposed acts of treason, although there were no proven cases of spying throughout the war years. Fanatical loyalists even objected to the public performance of music by German composers. Naturalised Germans lost the right to vote for the duration of the war.

Many Germans, regardless of whether they were involved in manual labour or had professional positions, were dismissed from employment or felt pressured to resign. Other workers refused to work alongside them. There were several strikes and protests.

Caught up in the war

During times of war, people close ranks against those they consider to be outsiders. Greek, Russian and Maltese residents were involved in various incidents during the war, revealing how quickly Anglo-Celtic Australians could reject 'foreigners' in their midst.

Two young Greek men posed for a photograph in 1916, shortly before they headed to the Western Australian goldfields. There in that year miners went on strike against the presence of 'enemy aliens' in the mines and townships and indiscriminately attacked any 'foreigners'. The original purpose of the photograph, handed down through the generations of a Greek Australian family, has been lost in time. It is known only as a photograph taken before the men got caught up in the Kalgoorlie 'race riots'.

In other incidents throughout the war:

On New Years Day in 1915 two 'Turkish' residents in Broken Hill attacked a train, killing and wounding local picnickers. One was then killed in return, the other wounded. In retribution, some Broken Hill townsfolk attacked the German Club and the 'Afghan' camel drivers' camp.

Greek residents were surveyed in 1916 in case Greece entered the war on Germany's side. This survey did not uncover any evidence of subversion, but became a detailed profile of Greek settlers living in many towns across Australia. They owned shops and restaurants. Others were canecutters, or owned their own cane farms. Some worked in the mining and fishing industries in Western Australia, or worked in the lead smelters at Port Pirie (SA).

In September 1916, during the first conscription campaign, anti-conscriptionists argued that the arrival of the *Arabia* carrying nearly a hundred Maltese men, was an attempt by the Australian government to replace Australian workers who would be conscripted for war service with 'cheap, foreign labour'.

In March 1919 left-wing Russian residents were involved in the 'Red Flag Riots' in Brisbane. The Red Flag, a socialist symbol banned during the war, was flown in protest at the Australian government's refusal to let them return to Russia where communist revolutionaries had overthrown the Tsar. They were attacked by counter-demonstrators, including ex-servicemen. There were injuries, arrests and deportations.

By war's end in 1918, 60 000 Australians had lost their lives and many others had been wounded. Australia had served the British Empire well.

1920s – 1930s
GRIM TIMES

After the war, the Commonwealth government, having assumed greater control over immigration matters, renewed efforts to attract immigrants.

Once again Australia sought its settlers from Britain while Britain saw emigration as a means to cement the bonds of Empire. The Australian and British governments offered subsidised passages and loans to cover remaining costs.

The White Australia Policy remained in force and the non-European population declined.

Enthusiasm for immigration was confined to the 1920s. Then in 1929 the world economies collapsed, bringing on the Great Depression. Immigrants who had arrived in the 1920s, attracted by Australia's promises of guaranteed employment, good wages and plenty of opportunities, faced economic distress, unemployment and poverty in the 1930s. They were grim times for the vast majority of all Australians and community attitudes hardened against immigrants. Emigration from Australia increased significantly. In 1929 assisted passage schemes closed.

A land fit for heroes

When Herbert Huxley was discharged from the Royal Marines at the end of World War I he was one of over eighty thousand British ex-servicemen who accepted their government's offer of a free passage to one of its colonies or dominions. Between 1919 and 1922 seventeen thousand headed for Australia with wives and children. Many of them took up land in soldier or group settlement schemes, alongside Australian ex-servicemen.

Herbert arrived in Fremantle (WA) with his wife and three children in 1921, and applied successfully to join the group settlement scheme in Pemberton (WA). A photograph of Herbert with his daughter Mabel sitting on the stump of a felled tree in a cleared and still smouldering forest patch reveals a glimpse of the hard life the Huxley family faced on their block. Most ex-servicemen and their families struggled to make a living, especially during the Depression, on small blocks, with poor soils, disappointing seasons, a lack of markets and high debt levels.

THE STARS WHICH SHINE OVER AUSTRALIA THE LAND OF OPPORTUNITY

THE "SOUTHERN CROSS"

THE CALL OF THE STARS TO BRITISH MEN & WOMEN

⭐ MEN FOR THE LAND
⭐ WOMEN FOR THE HOME
⭐ EMPLOYMENT GUARANTEED
⭐ GOOD WAGES
⭐ PLENTY OF OPPORTUNITY

FOR FURTHER INFORMATION APPLY TO ANY EMPLOYMENT EXCHANGE
OR TO THE DIRECTOR OF MIGRATION AND SETTLEMENT.
AUSTRALIA HOUSE. STRAND. W.C.2.

The call of the southern cross

Over 250 000 Britons, mostly English and Scots, resettled in Australia in the 1920s. In the post-war years in Britain, industries, such as mining and textiles, which traditionally had employed large numbers of workers, were declining. Many arrivals had relatives and friends in Australia who could nominate them for assisted passage. Church and community-based organisations, such as the YMCA, the Church of England and the Salvation Army also sponsored them.

Australian-based factories also nominated British workers with specific skills and experience. Paton & Baldwin's knitting mills in Launceston (Tas), producers of hosiery yarns and knitting wools, recruited skilled British textile workers in 1923. The workers hoped to secure their futures by transferring their skills out of a declining industry in Britain. And the knitting mill acquired experienced workers who could train local employees and recruit others from Britain, thereby ensuring the stability of its work force.

The Australian government still believed that the primary role of new settlers was to fill a vast and empty continent.

The families of Group 105 in the Kentdale area near Denmark (WA) were among several thousand British families who participated in Group Settlement schemes in the 1920s, mostly in the south-west of Western Australia, and on a smaller scale in Victoria. Family names included Holmwood, Bath, Wagstaff, Fiddler, Keeble and Hart. They came with hopes that, with hard work and good seasons, they would own a successful farm in Australia. They had varied backgrounds. Some were ex-soldiers; most were from British cities. On the whole, few had any farming experience. Even fewer were prepared for the tough life they encountered in the Australian bush.

Most immigrants reinforced the drift towards the cities that was already a feature of Australian settlement patterns.

Young men, such as this group arriving in 1926 in Sydney, readily found familiar types of jobs, as unskilled and skilled labourers, in factories, foundries and canneries in Australian cities and larger regional towns. In the first part of the 1920s factories in Australia expanded in number, producing the new consumer goods such as radios and vacuum cleaners.

Women were enticed to Australia with
promises of a future in Australian homes,
either as household servants or housewives.
Domestic servants were in constant demand.
Turn-over was high. Most young women
subsequently married or took jobs in clothing,
footwear and food processing factories.

Immigrants from Britain came from all walks of life, including the professions. Alice and William Granger arrived in Perth (WA) in 1926 wearing their Scottish kilts. Their father, John, a doctor and their mother, Daisy, a nurse, had both served in World War I. After the war, John established a medical practice in Oldham near Manchester, but after the death of his mother, the family decided to immigrate to Australia. They stayed for a while in Perth, eventually settling in Tottingham in Sydney.

This group of widows and children were typical of many British women who sought a new life in Australia after World War I had changed their lives. Many women had lost husbands and loved ones and had to relinquish employment taken up while men were at the Front.

Farm boys and child migrants

The Australian and British governments resumed their pre-war practice of bringing out young men to work as 'farm boys'. 'Orphans' from impoverished and neglected backgrounds were also resettled in Australia.

About three thousand 'orphans' came to Australia in the 1920s and 30s under the care of charitable organisations such as Dr Barnardo's Homes and Fairbridge Farms. The scheme was well-intentioned, aiming to give poor city children, most of whom had families unable to care for them, a fresh start and a better future. The boys were trained for farm work and the girls for domestic service. For some, it was a new start. Others were traumatised by the loneliness and emotional, physical and educational hardships they faced in an institutional upbringing in Australia.

The 'farm boy' schemes varied between the states. These boys were among over a thousand 'Barwell Boys' brought out to South Australia between 1922 and 1924 in a short-lived scheme instigated by Premier Barwell to replace the six thousand men lost to South Australia during the war.

In this group, fresh, young and hopeful faces turned to the camera. They had just finished a long voyage together during which time they had likely developed friendships and a sense of group camaraderie. But they were soon to be 'farm boys', working long hours on isolated farms which struggled in worsening economic times. They endured harsh living and working conditions. In many instances farmers failed to pay wages due to them. A number of boys committed suicide.

Meanwhile, Aboriginal children were increasingly removed from their families. In homes and institutions and in mission schools they were also trained to become farmboys and domestic servants.

True grit

Non-British immigrants, mostly southern Europeans, came without the assistance or encouragement the Australian government gave to British settlers.

Emigration from southern European countries was strong after World War I. A new and better life in America remained the dream for most of the young men who left their impoverished villages. But after the United States introduced immigration quotas in 1921, they looked to Australia in greater numbers.

The arrival of thousands of southern Europeans in the early 1920s worried the Commonwealth government. In response, it began to impose restrictions.

In 1924, the year that Frank Manicola from Malta applied for his passport to Australia, the government required southern and eastern Europeans to pay a landing fee of forty pounds or be sponsored by a relative already in Australia. In 1928 and in 1930 more restrictive quotas were set and the landing fee raised even higher. At the same time British immigrants paid only three pounds.

Many of the young men left with the intention of returning to their homeland. But like these two men who were the first settlers from the Italian village of Molinara to arrive in Adelaide (SA) in 1927, many stayed on, eventually bringing out their families and encouraging others to follow, leaving the village almost deserted of all but its older residents. By the end of the century there would be thousands of Australians 'descended' from these first two arrivals from Molinara.

With the number of reunited families increasing over the years, southern European settlers recreated the old village and regional networks in suburbs, towns and farming areas around Australia.

Government restrictions meant that new arrivals from southern Europe in the late 1920s and 30s were mostly wives, children and other immediate family members of men already resident in Australia. When Ida Sartori (2nd from right) arrived at Port Melbourne as a proxy bride in 1935 her sisters-in-law were there to meet her.

When Joseph Hamood's wife and children joined him in Australia in 1929 from Lebanon, she was one of just a few Lebanese who came to Australia in the 1920s, compared with the peak years of Lebanese emigration in the late 19th and early 20th centuries. 1920s arrivals generally contributed to the consolidation of families already in Australia. The Hamood family was part of the ebb and flow in emigration and immigration patterns.

Rocks, land, dirt and dust

Many southern European settlers took up unskilled labouring jobs, often in isolated rural areas, as their first step to forging a better life in Australia. During the Depression years, such work became a means of survival. Their hard labour contributed to the development of Australia's rural industries and transport systems.

Above: New arrivals helped to plant and bring in the harvests around Australia. In the late 1920s Italian settler Antonio Girolamo worked on a wheat farm to the north of Adelaide (SA). Many a new arrival followed the seasonal work available in Australia's agricultural districts.

They built roads and railways, toiling in the sun in remote country areas. Macedonian settlers, Evan Kiosses, sledgehammer in hand, and Tanis Radis, looking on, worked in a quarry near Cungena on Eyre Peninsula (SA). It was their job to break up stone for the railway line across the Nullabor. Italian settlers also mined the mica fields in isolated central Australia in harsh and difficult conditions.

Italian settlers Angelo, Giovanni and Albino Sartori worked on the construction of the Hume Weir in the late 1920s, after their previous place of employment, a Beechworth (Vic) tannery, had closed. The Hume Weir was constructed to provide irrigation to open up areas along the River Murray for closer land settlement. These areas attracted many settlers including southern Europeans.

The workers on this bridge project at Ballan, near Ballarat (Vic) in 1928 were mostly Italian, including the three Stella brothers. They worked a dangerous ninety feet above the river, with a boat moored below in case a worker fell in.

Skilled building, mosaic and terrazzo workers from Italy applied centuries of Italian tradition, knowledge and skills to the construction of Australian cities, public buildings and homes. Stonemason Arturo Comelli arrived from Italy in 1927. At first he worked on farms and built fences. Despite concerns raised by local trade unionists at the employment of 'foreign' labour, he found work in the late 1930s in his trade, carving the decorations on the stone capitals and frieze of the new Parliament House in Adelaide (SA). His name does not appear, however, on the lists of workers, his family believing that it was removed after he was interned during World War II.

Economic independence

Owning a business or farm symbolised the fulfilment of the immigrant's dream of economic success and independence in a new land.

In 1934 the Ferraro brothers had a greengrocery business on Eyre Peninsula (SA). In a truck laden with sheep, rabbit and fox skins for sale to Elders & Co, stock agents and wool merchants, they drove to Adelaide for supplies of fresh fruit and vegetables for their customers in this remote farming district.

Jose Paronella migrated from Spain in 1911 and after working first as a canecutter, acquired his own cane farm in Innisfail (Qld). In 1930 he retired and decided to build a Spanish castle, a reminder of home. It was his palace of dreams come true. In 1935 it was completed and soon became a tourist attraction, known as Paronella Park.

Years later the castle was badly damaged by fire, but the surrounding lands were converted to a picnic ground.

In Lygon Street, Carlton, a Melbourne suburb, M Fetter, a Jewish settler who had arrived from Russia in 1924 with only sixteen shillings in his pocket, established Fetter Hosiery Mills. By 1928 the factory was turning out two thousand dozen pairs of stockings weekly.

Italian settler Vincenzo Duble, shown here in 1937, ran a barber shop in Coburg, Melbourne, his clients coming from nearby areas where many Italian settlers lived. Back in Italy he had been a barber/surgeon, fixing bones and pulling teeth as well as cutting hair. But this was not permitted in Australia.

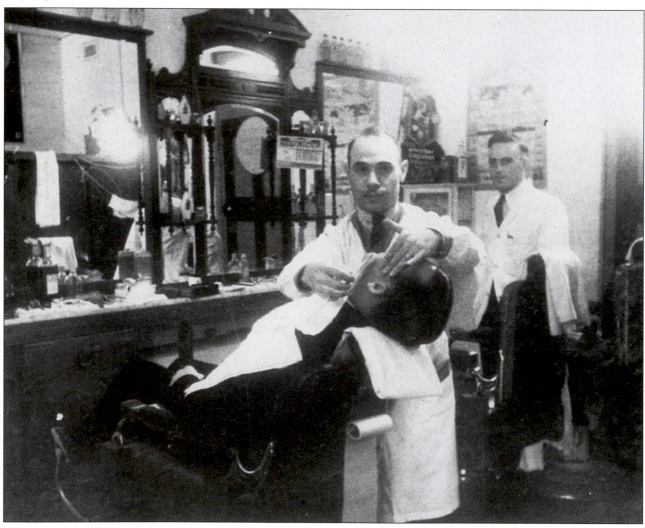

Photographs of cafés owned by Greek settlers are very common and perhaps disguise the fact that Greek settlers were also involved in many other aspects of Australia's economic life. Their cafés in hundreds of towns across Australia helped to create diversity in the business and social life of the towns. The Andronicus family had their Olympia Café in Allora (Qld).

Paul Coronakes was one of many Greeks who settled in the Lismore (NSW) district and became respected local citizens and businessmen. He was born on the Greek island of Corfu and settled in Lismore in about 1920. He owned and operated a fruit and vegetable store at several locations in Lismore and also ran a café. Here he is photographed with his staff in a shop he had on Keen Street in the 1930s. He was known as a quiet and dignified man who always gave his customers courteous service.

Pioneers on the land

Most southern European settlers had come from a village tradition of subsistence farming where extended families on small plots worked together to produce the household's yearly food requirements. In Australia they applied this knowledge and skill to commercial crops on properties close to markets in the capital cities and other major towns.

Anton Slavich left Dalmatia in the 1890s, living first in New Zealand before moving to Australia in 1924. He grew glasshouse tomatoes at Warriewood (NSW). He also ran a boarding house in the Rocks area in inner Sydney where many young men, newly arrived from Yugoslavia, stayed. In 1932 two new settlers, Ivan Vujnovich and Ivan Antunovich, worked on his property and stopped, buckets full, for a photograph as they harvested the ripe tomatoes.

THE CHANGING FACE OF AUSTRALIA

The Doceff and Staiff families, originally from Bulgaria, became market gardeners at Murray Bridge (SA). For this photograph, the women and children, dressed for a special occasion, stood in front of the packing shed, with the tins and packing crates stacked to one side. Family life on market gardens revolved around the business of growing, packing and selling. The involvement of women and children was as critical to the success of the farm as the men missing from the photograph. Over seventy years on, descendants still farm the land in the district, in a pattern of settlement common in many agricultural districts.

Extended families worked together. In 1936, on their farm at Ballandean (Qld) Giovanni and Rosarina Costanzo (standing at back), were given help to bring in the grape harvest, destined for the fresh fruit market, by their relatives (from left) Leonardo, Leonarda and Rosario Caruso and Rosario Pennisi, who had all come down to Ballandean from Innisfail to help out.

Ottavio Brida (first left) tried sharefarming with fellow Italian settlers on a tobacco farm in the Ovens Valley (Vic) to make a living during the tough years of the Depression.

Other immigrants to settle on the land included Russians who arrived in the early 1920s after the 1917 Russian Revolution. They took up cotton farming on land blocks offered for selection by the Queensland government in the Callide Valley. Mr Kolishkin, shown in 1936 pulling a plough behind a tractor, was one of about five hundred Russians who cleared the scrub country for cotton cultivation and established a close-knit farming community. Russian arrivals in the 1920s held political convictions opposite to pre-WW I arrivals. The earlier settlers were anti-Tsar and socialist in leaning; the post-war arrivals had been supporters of the Tsar and fought against the 1917 revolutionaries. After their defeat, they fled Russia, through China and Manchuria.

In the late 1920s Russians also settled in the Northern Territory at Katherine, where they pioneered peanut farming. Their names were Tokmahoff, Ivanetz, Krilov, Fomin, Zimin, Belokriloff, Sergeef… It was hard work and they battled poor markets, competition from Queensland, failing crops and uneven quality of the nuts. Numbers dwindled, the remaining farmers turning to vegetable and poultry production during the war years to supply the Australian army based in the Northern Territory. Disease and poor prices in the early 1950s spelt the end of peanut farming in Katherine.

Down through the years

The new arrivals of the 1920s and 30s worked alongside Australian-born workers and those who had arrived in earlier decades. In any immigrant society, layer upon layer of arrivals and their descendants interact, not necessarily on an equal footing, in the economic activity of their new homeland.

When motor transport made camel trains obsolete, 'Afghan' camel drivers turned to other itinerant work in outback Australia. This 1928 photograph taken in Broome (WA) showed an 'Afghan' settler making a living as a travelling cinematographer.

During the Depression, non-European residents were not entitled to government sustenance payments. Market gardening and hawking vegetables was at least a means of survival. By the 1930s Chinese market gardeners, such as this man at Bourke (NSW) in 1930, were ageing. Southern Europeans were moving into market gardening and younger Australian-born Chinese were taking up other occupations.

1920s – 1930s GRIM TIMES

Japanese pearl divers continued to work in northern Australia and in Broome (WA).

Diving for pearl shell was dangerous work. Many died. The Japanese cemetery at Broome became a memorial to the contribution they had made, with their lives, to Australian industry in the Top End. Australia became their permanent resting place, even if they were not welcome as permanent residents while they lived.

In 1931 Malay and Filipino crewmen from the pearling luggers were photographed as they were transported back to their island homes to the north of Australia at the end of their contracts. White Australia continued to dominate attitudes to non-European settlement in the twenties and thirties.

Molfettese fishermen, who had been arriving in the coastal town of Port Pirie (SA) from the Adriatic coast of Italy since the turn of the century, expanded the fishing industry in South Australia's gulf waters, establishing markets for their catches in Melbourne and Adelaide. Here they posed in the 1930s with other Australian-born fishermen on a Port Pirie wharf.

Jewish settlers from Eastern Europe had been orchardists in the Shepparton district since 1913. More arrived in the 1920s. Throughout the 20th century, seasonal work in orchards and canneries in the Shepparton district has attracted immigrants from many backgrounds, reflecting the changing origins of immigrant arrivals.

A farm in the bush: the group settlers

In the 1920s thousands of British settlers poured into the south-west forest areas of Western Australia. The state wanted to establish a dairying industry. With the Commonwealth, it opened up a group settlement scheme, offering assisted passages and loans to approved British applicants. The publicity said that they would own their own farm within five years. The scheme was not open to non-British immigrants.

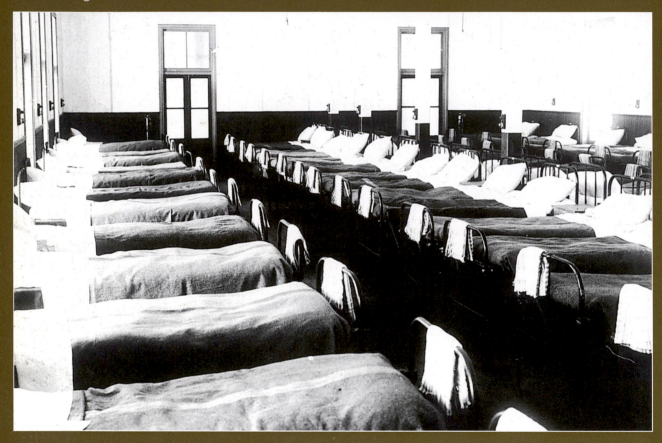

This line-up of closely-packed beds in the Immigrants Home in Fremantle (WA) was the first step many British settlers took in becoming farmers in Australia. There they were quickly allocated to farming groups, usually in lots of twenty blocks, and transported to the newly surveyed districts. There was a high turnover of arrivals in the Immigrants Home in the first busy years. The beds weren't often empty.

Accommodation was free for the first three days. After that, arrivals were charged a daily fee. This fee was on top of the landing fee of three pounds that all adults were required to pay. Other costs included the preparation of the farm site, a farmhouse, equipment and stock. All debts were to be paid back from earnings. With government assurances that the farms would be running successfully within a few years, immigrants started out confidently in debt.

Photographs reveal the daunting task facing the settlers. Group members were paid to clear at least twenty-five acres on each farm. They had to fell huge karri trees and cut down the dense virgin scrub. Usually the men were sent to do this job before their families arrived a few weeks later. During this time, the settlers lived in tents in primitive conditions.

After clearing the land, families moved into temporary tin shacks where they endured the extremes of summer and winter temperatures. There were no internal walls, with most families using hessian bags to make curtains for privacy. There was no running water. Parents lived in fear of their children becoming lost in the bush.

On each holding, government contractors assisted group settlers to erect a standard four-roomed house and basic fencing. It was then up to farmers and their families to make a go of it with their dairy cattle herds.

In 1926 the children of McLeod Creek lined up outside their first tin school. Two of the boys still wore the kilts of their Scottish homeland. Often children had to walk miles along lonely bush tracks to reach school. Most of the children had been born in British cities and the Australian bush, with its snakes and fires, held many fears for them. These children were probably recent arrivals as they were all wearing shoes. Children went barefoot after shoes wore out and were too expensive to replace. One teacher taught all grades, often using the bush to teach nature studies and drawing. The school was the only public building in the first years and all the dances, parties and meetings were held there. After school, children worked hard on the farm, milking and fetching firewood and water.

The sight of a car struggling to navigate its way along an isolated bush road typified the constant struggle that group farmers faced. Just over two thousand farms were settled, but it was hard to get goods to market or bring in supplies on poor roads, impassable after the frequent heavy rains.

On the whole, the scheme was a disaster, especially with the onset of the Depression. Farmers struggled against poor yields, poor soils, falling prices and failing markets. They sank further into debt. Without the means to improve their farms, they watched them deteriorate. Within a few short years, the government closed the scheme. Many group settlers abandoned their farms and left, heartbroken, with nothing to show for the years of grinding effort.

The group settlements were disbanded, but a nucleus of farmers remained. They expanded their properties, cleared more land and diversified into mixed farming, including pig-farming and vegetable production. After the Depression, farms began to prosper, local towns thrived and services expanded. Years later, telling the stories of the bitter struggles of the first settlers is left to the local museums and historical societies.

In the 1980s, the Southern Co-operative Butter Company building in Denmark, once part of the district's dairy industry from the 1920s to the 1970s, was reopened for use by a local winery. It also housed a craft shop and art gallery to cater for tourists who flock to the Margaret River wine region.

Anti-foreign feeling

The Depression hardened community attitudes against immigrants. Racism surfaced under the guise of protecting Australian jobs and businesses.

In the 1928 election, the Labor Party campaigned against continuing immigration. Although British arrivals were targeted, too, unions and employers focussed on preventing southern Europeans from taking up jobs that could go to Australian workers.

The Australian Workers' Union determined that only up to a quarter of a cane gang could be European and mining and manufacturing industries were reluctant to take on 'foreigners' as competition for available jobs intensified.

At the same time, European settlers belonged to trade unions that were heavily involved in strikes and other militant action during the Depression years. Croatian settlers, many of whom had socialist leanings, were a significant presence in Broken Hill's worker-based organisations.

The Spano family, settlers from Italy, were photographed in their fruit and vegetable store in Ascot Vale, Melbourne, in 1935. This had been their livelihood for nine years, having opened in 1926. They made it through the Depression years when Australian-born shoppers were widely encouraged to support their own first and boycott businesses owned by 'foreigners'.

Race riots

Anti-'foreigner' riots occurred on the Kalgoorlie goldfields in 1934. The death of a local Australian man in a fight with an Italian barman sparked the riots. Houses and property owned by or associated with southern European residents were destroyed. Three people were killed and many others injured. This was followed by strikes demanding employment preference for Australian-born workers.

Most photographs focussed on the extensive damage done to the goldfields township of Boulder during the riots.

One photographer, however, recorded the impact of the riots on the European residents. The photographer noted: 'An Italian family making a meal in a temperature of 110 degrees. Notice their home destroyed by fire'. Of the line of men, he wrote, 'The funeral of an Italian (sic) Katich. Notice all these men are without coats. Most of these people lost all their belongings destroyed by fire, barring those they are standing up in'. And of the Slavonic Dance Hall (top): 'Wrecked. This was not burned owing to being surrounded on all sides by Britishers'.

Keeping in touch

Immigrants in the 1920s and 30s maintained contacts, where possible, with people from their own villages and homelands. This contact was especially important during the Depression years when many were made to feel unwelcome.

184

This is a rare photograph showing almost all of the early Macedonian settlers in South Australia, gathered together in 1936 on the banks of the River Torrens in Adelaide to celebrate Christmas. On occasions such as Christmas, settlers made special efforts to get together. It was a time to remember past celebrations, to ease the pain of separation from family and familiar ways back home, and to celebrate anew in a new land.

Many Italians lived in the suburb of Carlton, Melbourne, in a vibrant close-knit community. Local parks and gardens provided a ready place to relax and gossip on a Sunday afternoon. Others liked to walk in the streets, greeting neighbours and friends as was the custom in the home country. Or they gathered at someone's home for a meal and a game of bocce, thereby establishing the basis for a more formal club in later years.

In the large communities, such as the Italian and Greek communities of Melbourne, Sydney and Brisbane, there was a lively, organised social life. There were gatherings to raise money for causes within the community itself, within the wider Australian society, or for their village and family back home. This 1933 photograph of members of Melbourne's Italian community gathered at the Cavour Club in South Melbourne for the Italian Red Cross Ball suggests a confident and well-established community life.

Marriage and religion helped consolidate community life and pass on tradition and custom. Here Rockhampton's (Qld) Greek settlers posed at the wedding breakfast at Economos Brothers' café, on the occasion of the marriage of their sister, Matina, to George Trifilis in 1925.

The extended family also helped to forge business networks. The Freeleagus family consisted of ten brothers, all of whom immigrated to Australia from Greece in the early years of the century, settling in Brisbane. By 1925 when this photograph was taken in front of a family home they were a well-known, successful and influential family.

Religion and education were important to the maintenance of cultural practices. At first Brisbane's Greek community used St Luke's Anglican Church for church services. In 1929 the community opened their own Greek Orthodox church. It was a proud day. The people in this photograph were mainly associated with the Freeleagus extended family. In the larger communities, too, it was also possible to establish schools for the children.

Chinese Progress Association
2nd Annual Ball
26/11/24

New land, new ways

Within settler groups, there is always diversity, change, interaction and adaptation in cultural practices.

The Chinese Progress Association held its second annual ball in 1924. Most of the young members were Australian-born, taking on Anglo-Australian cultural traditions. They were enjoying, as many Australians did in the 1920s, the popular black and white minstrel music imported from American vaudeville shows.

A Nazi flag raised not a flutter when Brisbane's German Club, the Deutscher Turnverein, contributed a float to the coronation festivities of Edward VIII in May 1937. The anti-German hysteria of WWI largely forgotten, they joined with other floats from the Royal Society of St George, the Loyal Orange Society, and from Irish, Welsh, Lancastrian, Scottish, Greek and Maltese residents. German organisations in Australia were generally not political or closely affiliated with the politics of Germany. They were mostly social, sporting and religious groups.

Some settlers participated enthusiastically in the popular sport of Australian Rules football. Mick Kanis, a Greek settler who arrived in Australia at the turn of the century, donated a cup to the Richmond (Vic) Football Club's Best and Fairest player at the end of each football season. The cup was presented at Kanis's café on Bridge Road in Richmond where there was a high concentration of Greek settlers.

British settlers brought their game of soccer with them. It was played especially in areas of concentrated British settlement such as on the group settlement farms in Western Australia. Here in 1923 British men working at the Gas Works in Brompton (SA) formed the Hindmarsh British Football Club and played against teams with names such as the Lancasters.

Southern Europeans brought with them a love of music and song. In moments of leisure and occasions for celebrations there was always someone who could play the treasured folk tunes on traditional instruments.

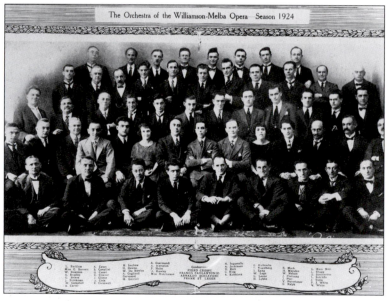

Others brought their classical music training and joined Australian orchestras. The Orchestra of the Williamson-Melba Opera Season 1924 included many players with Italian names. They joined with Australian-born, German and British players.

Sydney department store, David Jones, flew the Welsh flag on St David's Day.

Many Scottish settlers arrived in the 1920s and 30s and their cultural traditions thrived in Australia. Here a woman and her little daughter participated in Scottish celebrations in Sydney in the early 1930s.

Scottish dancing was a popular pastime in Australia in the 1930s, but it was not confined to Scots alone. Chinese sisters, Yvonne and Winsome Pang were prize-winning Highland dancers in the Wimmera district (Vic) in the 1930s. Their family and working lives were a far step away from the traditional lifestyle of their grandparents who had been born in China. Yvonne went on to teach music, elocution and dance with her sister Lorna. They put special effort into concerts which raised money for community services. They had learnt this sense of civic responsibility from their father, Harry Poi Pang, a herbalist in Warracknabeal (Vic).

On Remembrance Day, 11 November 1940, women of the Irish Grand Orange Lodge marched in procession on Sydney streets. The presence of Protestant Irish settlers in Australia tended to be over-shadowed by the more numerous Irish Catholics.

In 1929 Perth's Catholic schoolchildren celebrated St Patrick's Day in the botanical gardens in South Perth. Irish immigration slowed considerably in the 1920s and 30s after the Irish Free State was established in 1921. These children were most probably Irish-Australians, their Irish identity forged to a large extent through the Catholic Church. Many priests and nuns came from Ireland at this time to minister to Australia's Irish Catholics, reinforcing ties with Irish Catholicism. One of the greatest cultural divisions in Australia at this time was that between Catholics and Protestants.

Descendants of German settlers continued the traditions of their Lutheran faith. But children such as these girls at their Confirmation in Tanunda (SA) probably had less knowledge of the German language than their forebears. The restrictions on the use of the German language during the war years (1914-18) meant that English had become the language used in German Lutheran churches and schools.

This photograph of an audience seated in Broome (WA) for a picture show in 1920 graphically illustrated the racial divisions that existed in Australian society, especially in frontier towns. But it also highlighted the class divisions and the divisions between bosses and workers.

A diversity of people made up the audience. But they were deliberately segregated. The comfortable cane seats in the best location in the cinema were reserved for the lugger owners and other white Australian residents. The Japanese divers, the Asian boat crews and resident Chinese sat to one side and to the front on wooden benches. The Aboriginal audience found whatever spot they could at the back.

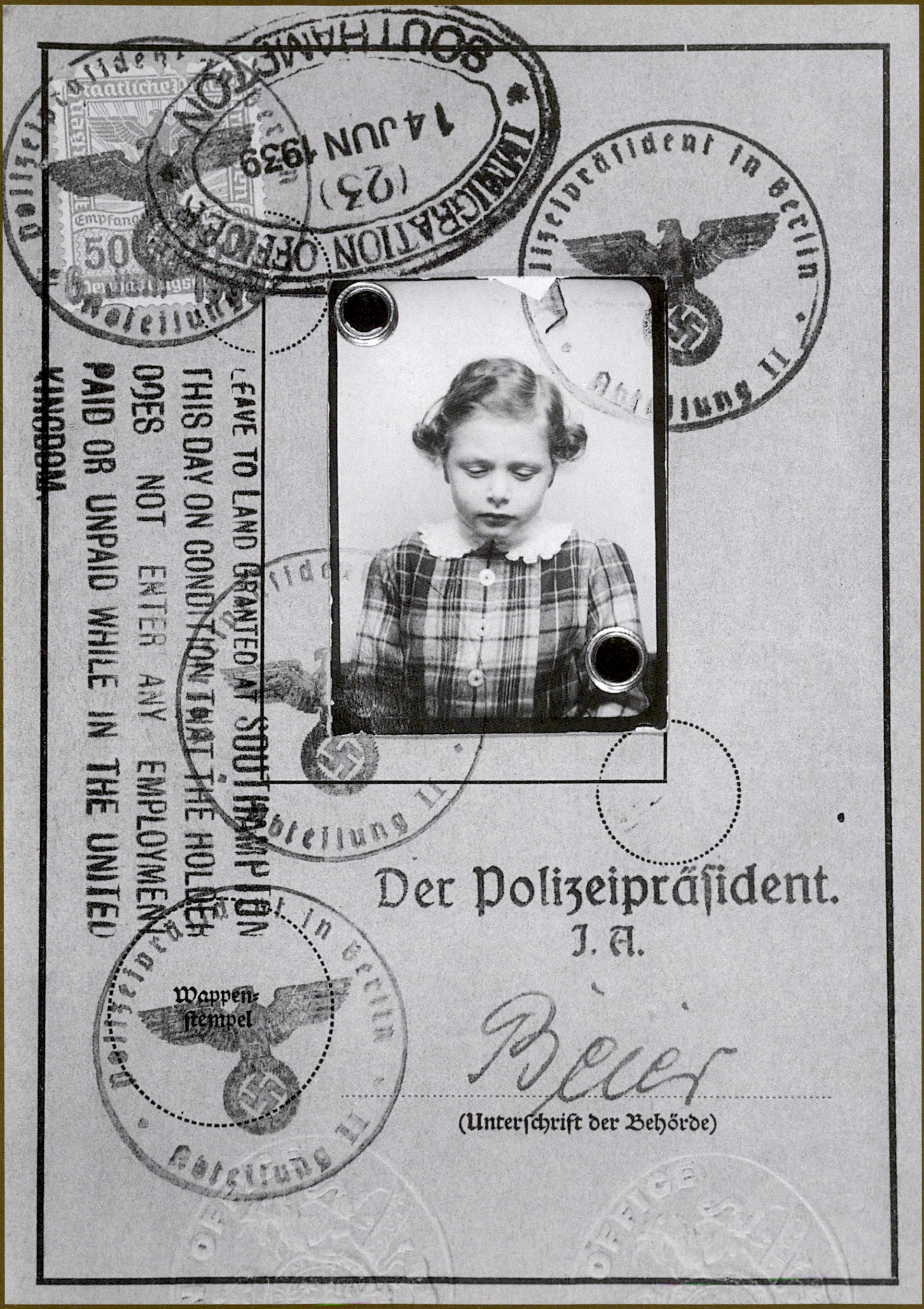

IMMIGRATION OFFICER
SOUTHAMPTON
14 JUN 1939
(23)
Polizeipräsident in Berlin
Abteilung II
LEAVE TO LAND GRANTED AT SOUTHAMPTON
THIS DAY ON CONDITION THAT THE HOLDER
DOES NOT ENTER ANY EMPLOYMENT
PAID OR UNPAID WHILE IN THE UNITED
KINGDOM
Der Polizeipräsident.
I.A.
Wappen-
stempel
(Unterschrift der Behörde)

The last arrivals

Few immigrants arrived during the Depression years. Australia did not encourage immigration and only at the end of the 1930s did the federal government re-introduce the assisted passage scheme for British settlers. Only a few thousand took advantage of the scheme before war loomed again. The thirties closed with the arrival of Jewish refugees from Europe.

Opposite: A little girl, her head bowed, her passport covered with Nazi stamps. She was one of about 5000 Jewish refugees who arrived in Australia at the end of the 1930s, settling mostly in Sydney and Melbourne.

They had fled their countries as Hitler's intentions against Jews in Germany and in the occupied areas of Austria, Czechoslovakia and Hungary became clear. In the 1930s Jews had faced dismissal from jobs, social restrictions, threats and attacks. Thousands fled across the Channel to the safety of England.

Jewish groups in Australia lobbied the Australian government to offer settlement to European Jews. At this time, the government was restricting immigration from Europe with quotas and high landing fees. It was not keen to reverse this decision, especially with continuing community disapproval of immigration. The lobbying was eventually successful and in 1938 the Australian government reduced landing fees and agreed to accept Jewish refugees who could be supported by Australian sponsors.

These new arrivals, dubbed 'reffos' by a negative press, were encouraged by the predominantly Anglo-Jewish community to fit in as quickly as possible to avoid stirring up anti-Semitism in Australia.

Many of the refugees were highly educated and talented. They went on to make significant contributions to the arts, the professions and academic life in Australia. Dr Steven Kinston fled Romania, arriving in Brisbane in 1938. A dentist by profession, he was also an accomplished pianist. In 1955 he established a Queensland branch of Musica Viva, an organisation formed by fellow Jewish refugee, Richard Goldner, in 1945 to promote chamber music. Steven also ardently supported the Queensland Symphony Orchestra and Brisbane Arts Theatre.

1939 - 1945
WAR AGAIN

Albert Que Noy was one of many men and women from Darwin's Chinese community who enlisted for service overseas. In later years he repeated with much humour the story of how he was shot at several times by fellow Australian soldiers in New Guinea when they mistook him for the Japanese enemy. He learnt very quickly to keep his slouch hat on at all times. Eventually he was posted back to Australia for his own safety.

For the second time in the 20th century, between 1939 and 1945, Australia was at war. Again, it responded to Britain's call to arms against its former Great War enemy, Germany. This time, though, the war was not fought largely on distant European battlefields. The war against another enemy, Japan, came closer to home.

The war affected many, if not most, Australians, but it had a particular impact on immigration and on overseas-born Australians. During the war years immigration schemes were abandoned as the government focused its resources on the national war effort. Arrivals dwindled and shipping concentrated on the movement of armed forces and goods essential for the war effort. The war also played a significant part in determining the future direction of Australia's immigration policies.

In the service of their country

During the war a million Australian men and women enlisted for service overseas. Many more performed essential services at home.

For some volunteers, their stake in Australia went back generations; for others Australia was a relatively new homeland. Those who served came from many backgrounds, reflecting over 150 years of immigration history.

It was not easy for non-European Australians, or for Indigenous Australians, to join up at first. The rules stipulated that recruits should have British or European backgrounds. Once the war directly threatened Australia's security this rule was increasingly ignored.

Doing their bit

When Greek Australian Spiro Polites (left) joined the Home Defence Labour Corps based at Tocumwal (Vic) he was one of many Australians of European background who volunteered to serve.

Frederick Malouf, son of Darwish Malouf, a settler from Lebanon at the turn of the century, served in the army during the war.

For Nellie Shu Ack Fong and her husband Thomas Slit Schin Fong, market gardeners at Pine Creek (NT), service in the war involved growing and supplying vegetables to the Australian Army based in Darwin. When Darwin and Katherine were bombed by the Japanese in early 1942, Nellie and other women were evacuated to Adelaide. Tom continued to work the market garden alone.

About three thousand Indigenous Australians also joined the armed forces.

Far from home

For Australians of British, Italian, Greek, Yugoslav, Chinese or other background, the war meant separation from their 'home country' and families overseas.

Many whose homelands had been attacked by forces opposed to the Allies raised money for the war effort in their former countries.

In October 1942 the *Courier Mail* photographed Chinese Australians collecting money in Brisbane's streets for medical aid for China. Japan had invaded China in the 1930s and fighting lasted there until 1945.

Melbourne's Greek community formed a branch of the Red Cross and organised fundraising events, including concerts for the Greek war effort.

These young Greek boys attended an Anzac Day service at Berrigan (NSW) in 1944. With the war, a new attitude to Greek Australians, often the target of anti-foreign feeling in Australia in earlier decades, emerged. Greek and Australian soldiers had become comrades-in-arms in the bitter, hard-fought but eventually victorious battles to repel the Axis powers from Crete and Greece.

The war interrupted the process of chain migration that had for decades linked immigrant settlers with their homelands and their families.

Nicolangelo Turci (right) came out from Molfetta on the Adriatic coast of Italy in the early 1930s to work in the large, close-knit Molfettese fishing community in Port Pirie (SA). Nicolangelo worked hard to bring his family out. But the war intervened and it was 1948 before his wife and younger children were finally able to sail for Australia. Tragically, his wife contracted pneumonia at Colombo and died as the ship sailed into Fremantle (WA).

'The enemy within the gates'

Australian residents whose home countries fought against the Allies came under police surveillance, had their freedom of movement restricted and endured the suspicion of neighbours. Some were interned.

With the outbreak of war, internment camps for 'enemy aliens' were established across Australia. Internees included German, Italian, Japanese and Hungarian residents. The first internees were German nationals, in particular those identified as having Nazi sympathies. About 2000 were interned in all. German clubs, at least those that had reopened after World War I, were again closed and German-language newspapers taken out of circulation.

Following Italy's entry into the war against the Allies in June 1940, nearly 5000 Italian nationals and others under suspicion were interned.

Some Italians in Australia in the 1920s and 30s belonged to the Italian Fascist Party. Others were anti-fascist. Still others wanted nothing to do with the politics of home. Here (below) members of the Fascist Party gathered in Sydney. In Melbourne (above) in 1929, anti-fascist group Club Matteotti protested on May Day against fascism.

Stefano Stefani came to Australia for the first time in 1925, finding unskilled work across Australia. He then worked as a carpenter in New Guinea, an Australian mandated territory, before returning to Italy where in 1939 he was drafted into the Italian army. After a short stint in Abyssinia and before Italy sided with Germany in 1940, he returned to New Guinea. In 1941 he was interned at Orange (NSW) and then transferred to Loveday. Later he wrote on the back of his ID photograph, '42 months in prison. An experience I can never forget'. Stefano was repatriated to Italy at the end of the war, but on seeing the poor conditions there, immigrated to Australia with his family.

Many internees went to Loveday camp (SA). Australian Army sergeant, Hedley Cullen, photographed the camp movements, working parties and leisure activities there. Here he recorded a group of Italian internees as they were moved from one compound to another.

Australian military authorities failed to identify and separate Italian internees who opposed fascism from those who supported Mussolini. As a consequence anti-fascist internee, Francesco Fantin, was murdered by another internee at Loveday in November 1942.

Many Italian nationals felt bewildered, angry and frustrated by their internment. Although some had belonged to fascist and anti-fascist organisations, they posed no real threat to Australia's war effort.

By the end of the war most Italian internees had been released to work on the land to alleviate the labour shortage. Not all Italians were interned. Many had become Australian citizens as war loomed. Some worked in industries or occupations deemed essential to the war effort. They thus avoided internment but remained under the surveillance of the local police.

In 1938 Italian settler Francesco Borgia opened the first pasta factory in Adelaide, Sovrana Macaroni Co. Proud of his Italian roots, he was also a long-time member of the local Italian fascist party. In 1928 he was photographed (right) in his role as standard-bearer. He was also the party's sporting director. When Italy declared war against the Allies on 10 June 1940, Francesco and other party members were interned. Although the factory was initially closed, the Department of War Organisation of Industry wanted it reopened to supply the local market. In June 1942 Luigi Crotti, Francesco's business partner, began production again. Borgia was released in January 1944 and resumed control of the factory. Crotti opened his own pasta factory, San Remo.

'I am concerned at reports I have received regarding the internment of aliens in my electorate. At Werribee, where there is a colony of Italians, the internment of many men has resulted in extreme hardship for their families. Their gardens – most of them are engaged in market-gardening – are running to seed. I presume that the internment of many of these men was a precautionary measure and that if, on investigation, it is found that they are law-abiding citizens, they will be subsequently released. If that is so, I trust that the matter will be expedited'.

John Dedman, local Member of Parliament for the Geelong area, in a letter to the Commonwealth government minister overseeing the internment of 'enemy aliens', 1940.

Other internees at Loveday and other internment camps included over a thousand Japanese living and working in Australia on temporary permits. Most were pearl divers in Broome (WA) and Thursday Island (Qld) when war with Japan broke out after the attack on Pearl Harbor, Hawaii, in December 1941. They remained in Loveday internment camp for the duration of the war, growing vegetables, raising pigs and producing opium poppies for morphine. This photograph shows them preparing to cut timber at Woolenook on the River Murray (SA). About a hundred Japanese women and children were interned at Tatura in Victoria.

Prisoners-of-war

Of the half a million Italian soldiers captured during the war, seventeen and a half thousand were held in prisoner-of-war camps in Australia. For some of these soldiers their brief interaction with the landscape and people of Australia was to change the course of their lives. After repatriation they came back to Australia as immigrants.

One of the biggest prisoner-of-war camps in Australia was at Cowra (NSW). Within its barbed wire perimeters were Italian, German and Japanese soldiers captured mostly in the North African and Pacific theatres of war. This photograph of a soccer match was taken late in the war or possibly in 1946 as the prisoners waited for arrangements for their repatriation to be completed.

In August 1944 Japanese prisoners-of-war at Cowra attempted a mass escape. Over two hundred were killed and a hundred wounded. Four Australian army guards were killed and others injured. The war cemetery there has become a permanent memorial and along with the Japanese Gardens is a major tourist drawcard, especially for Japanese visitors.

Giuseppe Magnavacca (left) was one of many Italian prisoners-of-war who were sent from Cowra camp to work on Australian farms. He worked with other prisoners on the Bartlett family's banana plantation in Middle Pocket, northern New South Wales.

By the time they were trucked back to Cowra for repatriation in 1946, they had almost become part of the Bartlett family. Giuseppe (holding baby) returned to Australia in 1951, sponsored by resident Italians whom he had met during his internment.

The Dunera Boys

A large group of Jewish refugees filed off the *Dunera* on 6 September 1940. But when they disembarked, guarded by Australian Army soldiers, they were regarded as 'enemy aliens'. In the late 1930s they had sought refuge from Hitler's Germany in England, and when war began in 1939, they were detained in England because of their German nationality. They were then sent to Australia for internment first at Hay (NSW) and then at Tatura (Vic). They were eventually reclassified as 'friendly aliens' and worked in labour corps to assist the war effort in Australia. Many remained in Australia after the war, making distinguished contributions to Australian society. They became known as the 'Dunera Boys'.

From war in Europe to refuge in Australia

At the end of the war much of Europe lay devastated. Millions of people were on the move. Most were ethnic Germans heading from eastern Europe to Germany after the disintegration of the Third Reich. Others were refugees, predominantly from eastern Europe. They had fled from advancing Soviet forces, or, having been detained in Germany during the war as forced labourers, were unable or unwilling to return to homelands that had fallen under Soviet control.

Lithuanians, Latvians, Estonians, Poles and Ukrainians, along with Hungarians, Czechs, Slovaks, Bulgarians and Yugoslavians crowded into Displaced Persons camps hastily established by the Allied victors in Germany, Austria, Italy and France. There they awaited resettlement.

Initially, from 1945 to 1947, Displaced Persons came under the care of the United Nations Relief and Rehabilitation Administration (UNRRA) which sought to repatriate as many as possible. When many refugees refused to return because of their fear of the Soviet communist regime, the International Refugee Organisation (IRO) was established to resettle the non-German refugees overseas.

Of the million or so Displaced Persons resettled overseas between 1947 and 1953, about 170 000 were accepted into Australia.

Displaced Persons had little to bring with them when they came to Australia. Most had lost everything during the war, including family photographs. Some arrived with a new set of photographs recording the steps they had taken in the camps to begin a new life.

In Fallingbostel Displaced Persons camp in Germany, Polish soldier, Franciszek Samojlowicz (right) was reunited with his daughter, Irena, after years of separation.

Many of the refugees were children. In the camps they began to play again after years of knowing nothing but fear and dislocation. These children were in Aufrauschule camp in Bavaria, Germany.

In the camps people met and married and children were born. In 1947 Janis and Emilija Aumalis celebrated the baptism of their baby daughter Vija in Spakenburg III camp in Germany. For many refugees the birth of a child was a sign of renewed hope for the future.

It was important to find work. Polish-born Franciszek Samojlowicz was a shoemaker by trade. He found work repairing shoes in Fallingbostel camp. Most of the people in the camps had very little, and new shoes were an unheard of luxury. The shoemakers in this workshop also repaired boots for United States Army personnel.

Other refugees began to study again. During the war they were forced to put career plans on hold. They also hoped that tertiary qualifications would increase their chances of being accepted for resettlement in another country. This group celebrating Christmas in 1947, were engineering students at Braunschweig Technical School in Germany.

Survivors of the Holocaust

Very few of Europe's Jews survived the war. They had been shot in forests, worked to death in labour camps and were systematically killed in the gas chambers of concentration camps. Although the exact number is not known, it is estimated that the Holocaust claimed six million lives.

The survivors emerged, emaciated and ill, from concentration camps. Most were anxious to leave a Europe that had largely let their people suffer and perish.

Some found refuge in Australia, bringing with them the burden of survival.

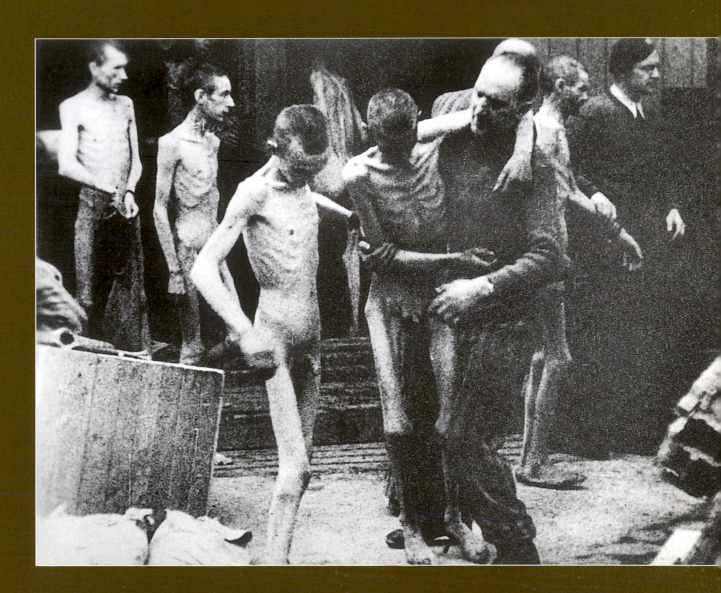

A place fit for heroes

At the end of the war Polish soldiers who had fought in the British armed services were unwilling and unable to return to their Soviet-controlled homeland. The British and Australian governments negotiated to offer them a new start in Australia.

Below: The Polish Carpathian Brigade joined British forces in Palestine in 1940. They fought with distinction alongside Australian soldiers in the North African campaign, earning the title 'Polish Rats of Tobruk'. In 1944, in the Polish II Corps (British 8th Army), they took part in the assault on German forces in Italy, in particular at Monte Cassino.

Above: Mieczyslaw Wolanski was one of many Polish servicemen who had fled Poland in September 1939 as the German army advanced. Fleeing through Romania or Hungary, they made it to France, joining the armed forces there. When France capitulated in June 1940, they fled to England, continuing the battle against Hitler in specially formed Polish units. Mieczyslaw became Leader of Polish Bomber Squadron 300 which fought with distinction in the Battle of Britain. Settling in South Australia in the late 1940s he worked for many years in the Commonwealth Government's Weapons Research Establishment.

It was this wartime event above all others that shaped Australia's post-war immigration policies. In February 1942 Japanese planes attacked Darwin. Australia's security had been breached. The long-held fear of invading hordes from Asia, the 'Yellow Peril', had become a reality.

At the end of the war, with Japan defeated, the Australian government was determined to strengthen the nation's manufacturing and industrial position and increase its thinly-spread population to protect Australia against any future threat of invasion. It was a matter of 'populate or perish'.

Only seven years ago a powerful enemy looked hungrily toward Australia. In tomorrow's gun flash that threat could come again. We must populate Australia as rapidly as we can before someone else decides to populate it for us.

Prime Minister Ben Chifley 1949

1950s – 1960s
VISION SPLENDID

'Populate or perish'

In order to protect Australia from external threat and create prosperity, the Australian government hoped to achieve an annual two per cent increase in population. It committed significant resources to a vigorous and sustained immigration program.

The result was that in the thirty years from 1945 to 1975 Australia's population almost doubled from seven and a half to thirteen million. Approximately three million immigrants arrived.

Initially, the Australian government assumed that its main source of immigrants would be the British Isles, Australia's traditional recruiting ground. But British immigrants made up only about half the intake in the 1950s and 60s.

The other half came from the European continent. This was a major break in policy for the Australian government which since 1901 had largely restricted its efforts and resources to recruiting British settlers.

In January 1947 the Prime Minister Ben Chifley (centre, with pipe) and the first Minister for Immigration Arthur Calwell (centre, with hat) greeted the first post-war assisted arrivals from Britain. The men were mostly building tradesmen. The Department of Immigration and the Commonwealth Employment Service were both established in 1945 and cooperated to recruit immigrants with skills required for Australia's economic development.

The Department of Immigration used photography extensively and exploited photo opportunities in the mass media. It wanted Australians to accept with confidence the arrival of large numbers of immigrants and to be enthusiastic about the brave new Australia that was being forged through immigration.

The Quest for People

Refugees brought from war-torn Europe between 1947 and 1953 under the Mass Resettlement Scheme for Displaced Persons were the first of the post-war non-British European arrivals. They, and others to follow, became known as 'New Australians'.

Australia's decision in July 1947 to participate in the huge international effort coordinated by the IRO to resettle Europe's refugees was made on humanitarian and economic grounds. In exchange for refuge in Australia Displaced Persons were obliged to enter into a work contract with the Commonwealth government for two years as unskilled labourers and domestics.

The first shipload of Displaced Persons landed in Fremantle on the *General Heintzelman*. There they were transferred to HMAS *Kanimbla* and arrived at Melbourne's docks on 5 December 1947. They then boarded a train for Bonegilla Reception Centre near the Hume Weir on the New South Wales-Victorian border. The photographer captured a wave here, a smile there, and faces, subdued and serious, as they began a journey into unknown territory.

With an aura of authority and confidence, Australian migration officers (from centre to right) Harold Grant, Bill McCoy and Frank Appleton posed for the camera as they supervised a trainload of refugees leaving from Augsburg camp in West Germany in late 1950. They and other migration officers sent to the Displaced Persons camps dotted across Europe were in a powerful position as they decided who to select for resettlement in Australia and who to reject. They were key players at a critical time in Australia's immigration history.

They were instructed to choose young single men and women in good health. The emphasis on suitability for labouring work meant that more men than women were selected and that a high standard of education or professional qualifications was deemed irrelevant.

Migration officers were directed by the Australian government to limit the number of Jewish refugees accepted for resettlement.

Only a few hundred Jews arrived as Displaced Persons. Most of the 25,000 Jewish refugees who made it to Australia, such as those on s.s. *Derna* docking in Fremantle in 1948, did so through the efforts of Australian Jewish relief organisations such as the United Jewish Overseas Relief Fund.

In 1945 Australian Jewish organisations had lobbied the government to help resettle Holocaust survivors. But lobbying from groups such as the Returned Services League and the Australian Natives Association, made the government wary. Jewish arrivals were restricted until the mid 1950s. Even so, Australia was second only to Israel, per capita, in accepting Holocaust survivors.

Ironically, in the chaos of post-war Europe when people could change identities or slip across borders, some war criminals involved in Holocaust atrocities avoided the system created to exclude them and arrived in Australia as Displaced Persons. Their identities have remained largely unknown. Only in the late 1980s did the Australian government establish the means to prosecute alleged war criminals. A number of cases came to court but charges were dismissed when evidence from witnesses was deemed unreliable fifty years on and the ill health of some of the accused made it difficult to proceed.

Between 1947 and 1953, over 170 000 Displaced Persons sailed for Australia.

Australia competed with other countries including Britain, Belgium, France, Canada, Brazil, Argentina and the United States for the refugees most capable of contributing their labour to economic development projects.

Only 35 000 Displaced Persons were Calwell's preferred 'Balts', made up of 20 000 Latvians, 10 000 Lithuanians and 5000 Estonians.

Other Displaced Persons included: 60 000 Poles, 24 000 Yugoslavs (mostly Croats, Serbs and Slovenes), 17 000 Ukrainians, 12 000 Hungarians, 10 000 Czechs and Slovaks, 3000 Russians, 2000 Germans, 1500 Romanians, 1000 Bulgarians

Others, in smaller numbers, were Albanians, Austrians, Danes, Norwegians and Swedes, French, Italians and Greeks. Some were classified as stateless.

The first refugees to pack their bags for resettlement in Australia were from the Baltic countries of Lithuania, Latvia and Estonia. They were chosen by immigration officials because they most closely resembled Anglo-Celtic people. This was done to reassure Australians, traditionally wary of 'foreigners', that they would blend in. Once in Australia they became known as 'Balts', a derogatory term derived from Immigration Minister Arthur Calwell's public emphasis on their Baltic origins. As more DPs arrived they too, regardless of nationality, were labelled 'Balts'.

The international competition for suitable labourers meant that from late 1947 Australia began to accept other nationalities and to include dependent wives and children of fit men. Families such as the Szillers, originally from Ukraine, departed for Australia in 1949.

Trains feature in many photographs taken by Displaced Persons as they headed for Australia. They were an integral part of the forced movement of masses of people across Europe during the war and the first leg of the journey for refugees seeking a new beginning away from war-torn Europe.

Displaced Persons endured difficult, cramped and primitive conditions on their voyage to Australia on board former troop ships chartered by the IRO. Their shipboard photographs, however, emphasised new friendships forged, the thrill of sailing through the Suez Canal, the Crossing the Equator party, or sighting Sydney Harbour for the first time.

'Ten British for every foreigner'

The intake of European refugees did not displace British immigrants from the top of Australia's hierarchy of preferred arrivals.

Shortly after war ended, Immigration Minister Arthur Calwell negotiated an Assisted Passage Scheme with the British government. This agreement operated for thirty years, albeit with diminishing commitment on the part of the British government, from October 1945 until 1975.

Most of the one and a half million British immigrants who entered Australia during these years came under the assisted passage scheme, nominated either by the Commonwealth or by private individuals and employer groups. Others came as unassisted immigrants.

The Australian flag flew at the stern of the *Oriana* as it left Southampton in 1962. It was one of a constant stream of chartered migrant ships that sailed between Britain and Australia.

On board these ships were British immigrants who had matched Australia's selection criteria based on work skills and health standards. For just ten pounds per adult, and children free, they were on their way to a new life in Australia.

Immigration Department photographers often recorded the experiences of families as they embarked for Australia. Recorded for posterity was the Millwood family from Sussex as they boarded the *Himalaya* at Tilbury Docks on their way to Victoria in 1956. Such gangway photographs were common.

The promotion of Australia emphasised its healthy lifestyle, with the sun, the surf and the beach, its modern cities and suburbs, education and job opportunities, full employment, good wages and conditions and a home of one's own to top it off.

At first, people left a bleak Britain struggling to recover from years of war. Damaged cities, housing shortages and a lack of basic goods and services enticed many to emigrate. To maintain the flow of applicants after Britain had recovered by the 1960s, Australia ran a comprehensive promotion campaign through its migration offices situated in major centres in England and Wales, Scotland and Northern Ireland. People lined up wanting to know more.

Bring Out A Briton

In 1946 Arthur Calwell counted upon ten British immigrants arriving for every one from Europe. It was an impossible dream and immigration ministers who succeeded him could at best achieve a fifty-fifty ratio. Even to maintain this level took effort. In its most imaginative and popular scheme, launched in 1957, the government urged Australian residents to do their bit and *Bring Out A Briton*.

Make it easier . . . help build Australia

BRING OUT A BRITON

This heavily promoted scheme relied on the public nominating friends and relatives in Britain for assisted passage. Employers could also nominate the types of workers they needed. In return, sponsors had to provide initial accommodation.

Local *Bring Out A Briton* committees were established across Australia. They identified job vacancies, assisted sponsors and recommended applicants to the Department of Immigration.

In April 1958 on board the *Orsova*, Alexander Downer, the Minister for Immigration, welcomed two hundred and fifteen passengers nominated by fifty-two Rotary clubs throughout Australia.

The Union Jack on the podium reinforced the Minister's message that the new arrivals were part of a 'united action to build this great British Commonwealth of ours, to make it even stronger and more respected in the councils of the world'.

Service clubs such as Rotary, Apex and Jaycees, were particularly active in the *Bring Out A Briton* scheme, giving their efforts titles such as 'Operation Fellowship' and 'Operation Opportunity'. This was a time when patriotic service to one's country was measured by a commitment to increasing the population.

The breadwinners in this group arriving at Fremantle (WA) on the *Canberra* in 1962, with the sponsorship of the Rotary Club of Western Australia, were building tradesmen, exactly the type of skilled workers Australia wanted. But it was a growing source of tension between Britain and Australia that skilled workers, trained at the expense of government and industry in Britain, were being 'poached' by Australian employers.

When the people of Terang (Vic) needed a new pipe major for their Scottish Pipe Band, they used the *Bring Out A Briton* scheme to recruit a pipe major from Scotland itself. Mr and Mrs MacArthur, of Aberdeen, and their two children were among a group of more than 1500 assisted migrants who arrived in Melbourne on the *Angelina Lauro* and *Fairsea* at the beginning of June 1967.

For Queensland's Centenary celebrations in 1959, the Catholic, Anglican, Presbyterian and Baptist churches, the YMCA, Salvation Army, Rotary, Apex, British Ladies' Club and the Royal Marines Association sponsored British migrants, in a unanimous show of approval for the benefits of population expansion.

The Ennis family from Belfast, Northern Ireland, were sponsored by the Presbyterian Church. Arriving with 438 other assisted migrants on the *Orion*, they were part of a long tradition of sponsored immigration to Queensland. In the 19th century the colonial government was the most active of all the Australian colonies in operating schemes to attract settlers.

The 'Nest Egg' Scheme

Another popular scheme designed to attract Britons was the 'Nest Egg Scheme'. Launched in 1959, this scheme allowed families with more than five hundred pounds sterling to apply for assisted passage without being sponsored or nominated.

The sale of the family home gave the Lester family of Hornchurch in Essex enough capital to qualify for assisted passage under this scheme and Leslie, Joyce and their four children left for Australia on the *Fairsea* in September 1964.

In 1996 Leslie and Joyce Lester sat at their kitchen table in suburban Melbourne reading through a family history written in 1989 to celebrate twenty-five years of life in Australia. In the book they had recorded what it was like to leave England.

Leslie: 'I had a good job. We were buying our own home. Financially we were all right, but with children of the post-war 'Baby Boom' growing up, work and housing were predicted to become scarce. According to the blurb, Australia was short of people and there was plenty of space, houses and good wages. Ilford Films, where I had been working for ten years, had a branch in Melbourne. I wrote to them and they said they would consider me for a job.'

Leslie: 'We hired a hall in Upminster for the traditional farewell party. As we left 7 Hubbards Close for the last time our neighbours stood in the street and sang *Once A Jolly Swagman*.'

Joyce: 'It was as if the packing cases had always been there. I es cut up the table tennis table to make a packing case. Boxes and cases became part of the living room furniture. We disposed of a lot of toys and furniture. We acquired an enormous second-hand fridge. When it was set up in Australia it was too small.'

Phillip: 'The reality of leaving home hit me when the form master presented me with a farewell card.'

Ann: 'Nerves set in when we went to Thame in the last week to see the relatives and say a last goodbye. Mum came out in a rash. Margaret and Phillip were sick and then Jane and I were sick the night before we were due to sail.'

Jane: 'I was still dry retching as we drove to Oxford Station.'

Margaret: 'Friends took us to Kew Gardens as there was quite a large Australian and New Zealand greenhouse there at the time. It was too hot for me and I fainted.'

Child migrants and farm boys

Shortly after the war, Australia and Britain resumed bringing child migrants to Australia. The children were sent to training farms and church-run orphanages, for long-term care and education. The wisdom of this practice was not questioned for some years.

In 1950 these girls were among a large group of children who arrived in Fremantle (WA) on the s.s. *Asturias*. They were going to a Catholic orphanage. Others on board were headed for the Fairbridge Farm School at Pinjarra (WA). They were among many hundreds of unaccompanied children resettled in Australia in the 1950s and 60s.

Most child migrants were not orphans. They had been placed in British welfare institutions because of family difficulties. Once in Australian orphanages, they were denied contact with parents and siblings in England. In 1987 English social worker Margaret Humphreys established the Child Migrants Trust to help them trace their families, many then taking emotionally painful journeys back home to England.

In a rather conventional pre-war approach to the peopling of Australia, the Australian and British governments also resumed assisting young British boys to settle in Australia as 'farm boys'.

These young men, arriving in Sydney in 1964, were assisted to Australia by the Big Brother Movement which operated mainly in New South Wales from 1925. They were among a record number of five hundred boys due to arrive in 1964. They went to the Big Brother training farm at Liverpool before being placed on farms or, in a move more attuned to Australia's urban work force, into industrial and commercial work. This scheme was voluntary and, once in Australia, the boys could nominate their families for assisted passage.

Going back

Return migration amongst British arrivals varied from a few per cent a year to over twenty per cent especially in the 1960s. Homesickness, the pain of separation from family, family illness or tragedy, or disenchantment with an Australia that failed to live up to expectations, were some of the reasons why people returned to Britain.

There were also the 'second timers'. In 1955 the Caffyn family immigrated to Australia for a second time. Their story was one of many used by the Department of Immigration in its bulletin, *The Good Neighbour*, to reinforce the message that life really was better in Australia.

'Conditions in England generally are so much inferior. To fellow migrants I would advise – beware of homesickness'.
Hedley Caffyn

The Good Neighbour, No 17, May 1955.

To alleviate homesickness, a scheme was devised in 1968 whereby airlines offered special deals to parents and relatives of British settlers to visit their families in Australia at half the usual cost of a return trip economy class fare. Mrs Nora Brookes of Warlingham, was among the first to take advantage of the deal to spend some time with her daughter Clare and see her four grandchildren in Perth (WA).

'A Balanced Intake'

From the early 1950s the Australian government negotiated immigration agreements with European countries.

With the Displaced Persons scheme coming to an end and the stream of British immigrants slowing, Australia looked to Europe. European governments believed emigration would help solve widespread economic problems and high unemployment, legacies of the 1939-1945 war. Governments also faced a population crisis caused by a post-war baby boom.

People left Europe to escape unemployment, poverty, lost opportunities and lives disrupted by war. Family members and village and town neighbours dispersed around the world, establishing emigrant communities in places including Australia, New Zealand, Canada, Argentina, Brazil and the United States.

The flags of Australia and the Intergovernmental Committee for European Migration (ICEM) flew together above German and Austrian immigrants as they left a processing centre in Germany in 1956. Moving people out of Europe was a joint effort for mutual benefit.

Above: The Dutch government assisted in the departure of a million of its citizens in the 1950s and 60s. The Versteegens and Simonis families, arriving on the *Fairsea* in October 1955, were two of many large families among 125 000 Dutch making Australia their new homeland.

Below: A crowd farewelling their loved ones on a Naples wharf revealed some of the intense emotions associated with emigrating, for those leaving and those remaining behind.

By the 1960s Europe had recovered from war and the
European Economic Community (EEC) had created prosperity.
But people still responded to the promotion of Australia as a
land of opportunity, especially for children.

Like many others, Oscar and Lucie Dhyon of
Anderlecht in Belgium who arrived on a
chartered Qantas flight from Brussels in 1962,
were motivated to immigrate to Australia by
the prospect of a brighter future for their ten
children.

Treading warily

The Australian government trod warily in its new venture into Europe. It was anxious to maintain what it termed 'a balanced intake' that would not threaten Australia's Anglo-Celtic identity and culture.

This meant that, after British immigrants, the Department of Immigration preferred Dutch, West Germans, Danes and other western and northern Europeans in the belief that they would blend into Australian society and not form conspicuous minority groups.

The immigrants least preferred by Australian immigration officials were southern Europeans. Australia did not want to openly discriminate, so migration officers used discretionary powers to limit assisted passages for southern Europeans.

While about eighty-five per cent of British and seventy-five per cent of German immigrants were offered assisted passages to settle in Australia, only a third of Italian and Greek applicants were granted assistance.

Of the southern Europeans who qualified for assisted passage most were likely to be young single men, generally unskilled, whose labour was thought likely to benefit Australian industry.

With their departure for lands afar, these Italian men on board the *Fiorenzia* in 1952 were continuing a pattern of emigration from southern Europe unchanged since the 19th century. They were hoping to make a better life for themselves and their families left behind in the villages. Many intended to return home one day.

Emigration is a risk. Shortly after Italy and Australia signed their immigration agreement in 1951, the Australian economy temporarily slumped. New arrivals in migrant camps such as Bonegilla (NSW) had few prospects of getting jobs. Unrest occurred and the agreement was suspended for a time. The Australian government responded by setting immigration targets year by year according to economic circumstances.

Single women from southern European countries also qualified for assisted passage if their labour, too, was thought to be of direct benefit to Australia.

Most, such as these Greek women being processed by immigration officers after flying in to Melbourne in 1962, were recruited to work as cleaners in hospitals, homes, offices and schools. Little had changed for women since the early years of the century when young British and Irish women were similarly recruited. Women from Greece, Yugoslavia, Spain and Italy were selected only after other women, from Britain and western and northern Europe, showed limited interest in domestic work.

Many of the young women were from small rural villages and prior to departure they undertook training organised by ICEM to familiarise them with the modern appliances they would have to use in Australia.

These young women from northern Spain were featured in *The Good Neighbour* bulletin in April 1960. The caption told the story. 'Twenty-two Spanish senoritas arrived in Melbourne aboard a charter Britannia aircraft last month – the first of 100 Spanish single girls who will migrate to Australia by June 30.

The girls went straight to jobs as domestics in Adelaide, Melbourne, Sydney and Brisbane. Announcing their arrival, the Minister for Immigration, Mr A R Downer, said: 'Most of the senoritas come from northern Spain, which is proving an excellent recruiting ground for migrants. These girls are part of our drive to even up the balance of sexes in Australia.'

Bride Ships

With large numbers of single Italian, Greek and other southern European men arriving it was often hard for them to find a girl from the home country to marry. Many found it lonely living in boarding houses. Some married Australian girls as they learnt to speak English and gained confidence in the wider Australian society, or they met girls from other immigrant backgrounds. Often, though, their families back home helped them to find suitable marriage partners.

Especially in Italy, the bride went through a wedding ceremony with someone, often a brother, standing in, as proxy, for the groom in Australia. Hundreds of proxy brides then sailed to Australia, often nervous and fearful of what lay ahead. Proxy brides arriving on 'bride ships' became a common sight on Australian wharves.

An Immigration Department photographer captured a poignant moment when the *Aurelia* berthed in Cairns in 1956. Angelo Galleazzi dashed to the ship's side to greet his proxy bride, Lina. They had been married by proxy in January 1954 when Angelo was working in the canefields near Cairns and Lina was at San Justino in Italy. The caption went on to say that 'when Angelo waved to her, Lina was at first too timid to come down to the porthole to greet him. She stood at the rail half smiling, half in tears.' A little later, the photographer recorded them clasping hands for the first time.

Koula's story

Koula Aslanidis left her small village of Roditi, near the town of Kozani in northern Greece in February 1959 to marry Angelo, her next-door neighbour who had gone to Australia in 1954.

He had written home asking his sister to find him a wife. She asked Koula who took over a year to consider this proposal. She said yes.

Left: The people of the village came out to farewell her as she left by cart with her family and Angelo's relatives to catch the bus that would take her on the first leg of her journey to Australia. On the back of a photograph sent to her later were the words, *This is to remind us of the last few minutes before the bus will take my sister Koula far away.*

Right: It had been agreed between the families that if she did not like her fiance, whom she only slightly remembered, or Australia itself, she would be free to return home. Her fiance met her when the ship docked in Melbourne. They travelled to Adelaide and after spending a few months getting to know each other, they married in the Greek Orthodox Church of Saints Michael and Gabriel in June 1959.

Prisoners-of-war return

Australia was not an unknown destination for Italian settler Giuseppe Guidotta when he arrived in Australia in 1950. His first taste of life in Australia had been in 1944 as a prisoner-of-war.

After a time in detention camps, Giuseppe worked on the O'Dea property farm in Tintinara (SA). In late 1946 he was repatriated to Italy, but soon returned to Australia, this time with his wife and son, because 'the conditions in Italy after the war were deteriorating.' Mr O'Dea sponsored him and paid for the cost of the voyage, a sum that Giuseppe paid back. At first Giuseppe worked in the Tintinara district and built his first home there for his growing family. When this photograph was taken in 1962 he was working in the timber industry at Nangwarry, also in South Australia's South-East region.

Chain Migration

With families split between Australia and Europe, family reunion became as much a powerful motive for immigration to Australia as promises of jobs, sunshine and surf. It was also a key factor in the often high rate of return migration.

Ironically those most drawn to Australia by the strength of family and village ties came from the Australian government's least preferred source, Italy and Greece.

Families were separated, sometimes for years. In Australia, it took time to save up, get a house ready and send money home for the cost of the journey. Back in Europe, wives and daughters sometimes had to stay in the village to look after older family members. It took time to get through the selection process.

Three generations of women and children from a family of the small Italian village of Molinara were finally on their way to join sons, husbands and fathers already in Australia. This happy scene masks the difficulties faced by many southern European families. Throughout the 1950s and 60s migration officers restricted family reunion, especially for extended family members, and curtailed the numbers of assisted passages. As a consequence, southern Europeans generally arrived unassisted, paying for their own passage and relying on village and family networks for support on arrival.

Many photographs captured the excitement and tenderness of reunion. In 1951 Paula Ferraro, aged 82, left Italy for the first time to be reunited with her five sons who had earlier settled in Adelaide (SA). To her joy, her sons had prospered in Australia, owning a large quarrying and ready-mixed concrete business.

The Voyage

For some immigrants the sea voyage to Australia was an adventure and the holiday of a lifetime. For others it was a nightmare of seasickness and a wrench from the familiar. But, in an age when hand-held instant cameras became commonly-owned consumer goods, just about everyone who came to Australia by ship took a photograph or two to remember it by.

Official photographs taken by the Department of Immigration promoted 'the luxury facilities', such as children's play areas, on board migrant ships.

In 1964 the Lester family were on their way to Australia on the *Fairsea*. The souvenir photograph of a fancy dress party showed that they were having a good time. But the photograph tells only one story. As they wrote with humour in their family history:

'A cruise through the Mediterranean, through Suez and the Indian Ocean sounds romantic, idyllic, restful. Now let's get back to facts. The cabin was so small that there was only just room for all six occupants to stand at one time… The ship was crowded with 1200 passengers and crew. Deckchairs and bodies lined every available piece of deck space. Everyone set about enjoying themselves as well as any tin of sardines can'.

Most voyage photographs show parties, formal dinners, day trips at ports of call, swimming in the pool and new friends. Or the simple pleasure there was for German immigrants Elisabeth Etienne and her daughter Karin in playing ball on the deck of the *Castel Felice* on its way to Melbourne in 1956. For baby Karin, too young at the time to store up her own memories, photographs such as this are an important piece of historical evidence that she was a part of Australia's immigration history.

THE CHANGING FACE OF AUSTRALIA

A photograph of German immigrant Helene Sandl bending over a sink to wash clothes on the s.s. *Aurelia* en route from Bremerhaven to Australia in 1960, provides a rare glimpse of the ordinariness of life on board the migrant ships. Housekeeping jobs had to be done, especially by women, despite the adventure of travelling across the world.

The numbers game

The 100 000th Maltese arrival, the 250 000th Italian…
The Australian government publicly celebrated each
significant milestone in the immigration intake.

Austrian Eugene Mori was chosen as the
250 000th migrant assisted by the Intergovernmental Committee for European
Migration. He arrived in Melbourne on the
Skaubryn in November 1954 to be greeted by
the Minister for Immigration, Harold Holt
(right) and the former Minister, Arthur Calwell
(centre). Holt and Calwell belonged to
opposing political parties, but regardless of
which party held government the commitment
to the immigration program throughout the
1950s and 60s remained largely the same.

There was a great deal of fuss made when
Barbara Porritt, from Redcar in Yorkshire,
England, was chosen as the one millionth
post-war migrant. She arrived in Melbourne
with her husband Dennis, on the *Oronsay* in
1955. She was young, attractive, and British.
She perfectly matched the government's
image of the type of immigrant most
acceptable to Australians. Photographs of her
and Dennis settling in to their new life in
Australia were in all the papers. Here she looks
over the rebuilding of the Melbourne Cricket
Ground in preparation for the 1956 Olympics,
an event which the Australian government
used extensively to promote the benefits of a
vigorous immigration program.

Giuseppa Filiciotto from Sicily was the 50 000th migrant assisted by the International Catholic Migration Commission. In December 1964 the Commission gave her a free passage to Australia to mark the occasion. Since its formation in 1952, the Geneva-based Commission had lent more than ten million pounds to people migrating from countries including Italy, Spain, Yugoslavia, Germany, Austria, Belgium and Poland.

In the 1960s the social and religious divisions between Catholics and Protestants still ran deep in Australian society. Not everyone welcomed Catholic immigrants, fearing that continuing immigration from largely Catholic countries in Europe would significantly alter Australia's social fabric that had since settlement been based on a predominance of British Protestants.

The 100 000th Dutch arrival, Adriana Zevenbergen who came out in 1958, was photographed again in 1963, when her third son, her first Australian-born child, was born. The story emphasised how happy her family was in Australia. Mr Zevenbergen, an engineer, was earning thirty-two pounds a week. They were paying off a mortgage on a three-bedroom brick veneer house in Geelong (Vic). They were about to buy a car. The children were happy at school and liked Australian Rules football. They were a success story promoted by the Department of Immigration at a time when it was getting harder to maintain high immigrant numbers.

Welcome to Australia

Migrant reception centres, also termed hostels, holding centres or more commonly migrant camps, were the first taste of life in Australia for Displaced Persons and many other assisted immigrants and refugees.

The number of hostels varied according to need, but in the late 1950s over thirty operated across the states. Most were former military barracks refurbished to accommodate thousands of new arrivals until they found employment and a place to live.

The migrant centres were operated by the government instrumentality, Commonwealth Hostels Ltd. Many of the directors, shown here at a conference in Canberra (ACT) in 1953, had been military officers. This is not surprising. New arrivals were like an army on the move. It was a logistical effort to transport them, feed them and bed them down.

At Bonegilla, the first hostel established for Displaced Persons near Albury-Wodonga on the New South Wales-Victorian border in 1947, there were rows and rows of corrugated iron army barracks.

British arrivals encountered old woolsheds with chicken wire and tar paper for walls (and rats, remember former residents) at Rosewater, an Adelaide (SA) suburb, in 1951.

On a number of occasions, residents in Australian hostels held protest meetings about the poor standard of accommodation that failed to match expectations raised by migration officers overseas.

We were put into huts and sheds made of corrugated iron and bituminous felt. Previous tenants had poked holes in the paper felt and you could see and talk to your next door neighbours. The laundry and toilet blocks had gaps at the tops of the walls. The wind blew through in the wintertime and it was very hot in summer. There was hardly a blade of grass between the huts. I remember the dust and the mud. My mother never stopped talking about wanting to go back home.

English immigrant Derek Taylor, recalling eighteen months at Finsbury Hostel, Adelaide, 1951

There was little privacy in the single women's quarters at Kensington migrant reception depot in Sydney (NSW) photographed in 1951.

English settler Shirley Taylor waved to her husband Derek as he photographed her bringing in the washing at Adelaide's Gepps Cross hostel. They lived there in 1957 while they built their own home. In 1999 they recalled the living conditions as 'basic but comfortable enough'.

Bathrooms, toilets, showers and laundries were in communal blocks. Although the laundry facilities at Bonegilla in 1949 looked rather spartan, they were not a lot different from those in many Australian homes at the time.

Cooking food was forbidden in the huts. Everyone lined up together for the same food and ate together in large dining huts, such as this one in the 1950s at Finsbury (SA) shown decorated for Christmas.

'The butcher is an important man at any hostel. This one is at Villawood Hostel, Sydney', says the official caption for this 1957 photograph. Many European arrivals found it hard to adjust to the Australian preference for lamb. Endless meals of lamb chops turned many a stomach. Stories abound of people sneaking food and primitive cooking equipment into the huts to try to create the tastes of home.

Hostel living was a shock introduction to Australia for many arrivals. Most left the camps as soon as they could, although this was not always easy in the 1950s when there was a critical shortage of houses and building materials.

Corrugated tin Nissen huts astounded many British and European arrivals. Tin was, however, a common building material in Australia. It was cheap, easy to transport and fast to build with. Small, corrugated tin houses, hot in summer and freezing in winter, were home for many Australian workers and their families. This family home in Port Pirie (SA) in 1965 was one example. Nissen huts were a first home for many rural families, including soldier settlers.

Not everyone had the solid red brick houses, with garden and garage, shown in publicity posters enticing immigrants to Australia.

Improvements at hostels over the years were mostly superficial. In 1965 in Bonegilla an outdoor seating area with umbrellas was installed. The major changes occurred when the government built family units, such as those at Villawood, Sydney, pictured at right in 1969. These 'new look' units included a bathroom and toilet, although laundry facilities were shared. There was no kitchen. Families still had their meals in a common dining hall. But at least there was greater privacy.

When Polish immigrant Sev Ozdowski arrived at Villawood in June 1975 he was very happy with the facilities provided. 'For the first time in my life I had a room to myself.' But the food? 'After one week there we'd had enough'.

For the first shipload of Displaced Persons, there was time in the summer sun in late 1947 to play music beside the waters of the Hume Weir.

Life goes on

Many photographs of hostel life in the 1950s and 60s showed new settlers making new beginnings. Making friends, getting married, learning English...

Over 300 000 assisted immigrants and refugees stayed at Bonegilla (NSW) between 1947 and its closure in 1971. It was the main processing centre for Displaced Persons and there they began to make up for time and their youth lost to war in Europe.

Displaced Persons took personal photographs that emphasised new and curious encounters with their adopted country, a place they knew little about before their arrival. In 1949 at Bonegilla, Estonians Ene-Mai Prima (later Reinpuu) and Alfred Tuisk had a close look at the first snake they'd seen in Australia.

Other photographs depicted the rites of passage which mark people's journey through time. In the early 1950s Mike and Stefania Reimer had their wedding at Woodside (SA).

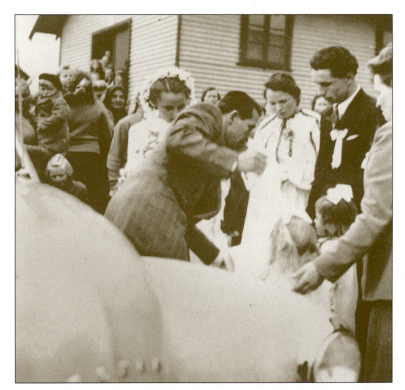

Displaced Persons were required to attend English classes while they were resident in hostels. This photograph showed an English lesson in progress at Woodside hostel (SA) in 1952. Only women and children were there. The men, whether single or married, were at work camps near large construction projects or factories. Wives and children were sent to special holding centres, such as Greta and Cowra (NSW) and Woodside (SA) to wait out the two years of their husband's contract. Many families felt anxious and resentful about this, as they had often endured separation in refugee camps in Europe and on the voyage to Australia.

The baby boom

In the 1950s and 60s Australian towns and suburbs were brimful of children. This was the era of the post-war 'baby boom'. Young arrivals, and babies born to new settlers, added significantly to the numbers of children.

Opposite: In hostels children celebrated milestones such as birthdays and events in the religious calendar. English settler, Heather McCooke recorded her child's birthday party at Rosewater (SA) in 1951.

Pre-schools, such as the one at Bonegilla shown here in 1955, were essential for many migrant mothers. It gave them the chance to work, adding to the family savings to build, buy or rent a home. Permanent work was difficult to find, though, especially near camps in rural areas. Women often had to be satisfied with seasonal work on local farms, or employment in the camp kitchens and offices.

Some of the larger hostels had their own primary schools, while older children were bussed to local high schools. At the school in Wacol hostel (Qld) children lined up for their free bottle of milk. At this time most Australian school children received free milk daily. This practice was promoted to potential settlers as proof that in Australia children would have all the ingredients for a full, healthy life.

Rosa's story

In the schoolrooms and playgrounds of Australia migrant children and Australian children sorted out their differences and found things in common. Many migrant children remember the cut and thrust of the schoolyard where they were teased because of their different clothes, food and accents.

In January 1962, when she was five, Rosa (on left) came to Australia from Spain's capital city, Madrid, with her parents and sister. Sorting through family photographs nearly forty years later evokes memories both painful and joyous for her.

'When I started school at Bonegilla I couldn't understand a word. I was the only Spanish girl in that class. I wrote cursive and the teacher pointed at me to print. I remember thinking that Australians must be morons. It was very frustrating because back in Spain I was reciting poems, sewing, doing Maths and writing stories. The teacher seemed to assume that I had no skills or knowledge because I didn't speak English.'

'This photo was taken at Bonegilla. We're still dressed like Madrid children. The photo was taken to send back to our grandparents and uncle and aunt to show how happy we were in Australia. We're wearing short skirts, woollen tights and white leather boots. When we started school in Whyalla (SA), where Dad worked at BHP, we were initially teased about our clothes. My mother couldn't understand it as these clothes were from fashionable children's stores in Madrid. My sister and I quickly learnt English and how to fit in and henceforth experienced very little direct racism. This, however, wasn't always the case with some of our other Spanish friends whose accents and appearance was more distinctive.'

'This was taken on a Sunday on the beach in Whyalla. In Madrid we went *de paseo*, for a walk on Sundays. For the first few years in Australia we continued this tradition. Mum would stay home and cook the Sunday *paella* and Dad would take us out somewhere. I remember Dad saying how back in Madrid there were beautiful things to see. At first we always dressed up on a Sunday, the way we had done in Spain. Dad would wear his suit, especially if we were going to take photos to send back to the family.'

'This photo also reminds me that we often felt different not only from Australian kids but from other Spanish children in Whyalla who were mostly from the south of Spain. We were city children with different accents, customs and clothes. Mum liked to keep us in pants and we never owned a flamenco dress like the other girls.'

'This is taken in the Spanish Club in its early days, in the mid 1960s, in Whyalla. The Spanish community would get together and have parties. People were close and stuck together. They were amazing parties. Lots of singing, dancing and flamenco. It was about paying homage to being Spanish. Dad, on the right, was a great admirer of flamenco. Children were never left at home. We had a great time.'

A 'home' life

Official Department of Immigration photographs painted a rosy picture of life in Australia for British child migrants. Such photographs were largely for the consumption of well-meaning Australians, but masked a different reality for many of the children.

The boys at Melrose Home near Parramatta (NSW) in 1953 are shown in a cosy and comfortable lounge room, contentedly playing games, reading and listening to the radio.

A photograph of the boys' dormitory at Fairbridge Farm at Pinjarra (WA) reveals a more spartan existence.

It is only since the 1980s that former British 'orphans' have spoken out about the emotional, physical, sexual and verbal abuse they endured, and the physical, social and emotional deprivations they suffered in Australian orphanages and training farms during the 1950s and 60s. They have sought compensation through the courts and won apologies from governments and church groups formerly responsible for their care, but the scars remain.

Photographs rarely reveal emotional deprivation, loss, abuse and alienation.

At the same time, many Aboriginal children were coerced into institutions, separated from their families, their communities and their culture. In the 1990s these girls pictured at Cootamundra Home in the 1950s in New South Wales and others like them, became known as the 'Stolen Generation'.

In 1997, *Bringing Them Home, The Report of the National Enquiry into the Separation of Aboriginal and Torres Strait Islander Children From Their Families* was handed to the Commonwealth Government by the Human Rights and Equal Opportunity Commission.
It acknowledged the pain and loss the children and their families experienced and recommended actions to redress the wrong doing, to link up children with their families and communities and to make restitution.

From many places

In the 1950s and 60s people came from a number of countries, although in smaller numbers than immigrants from Britain and Europe.

They came from Turkey after Australia and Turkey signed an immigration agreement in 1967. When the first Turks flew into Sydney from Ankara in 1968, Turkish Cypriot residents welcomed them with signs describing Australia as the 'ideal country of the day'. Perhaps it was, but the predominantly Muslim Turks found that they were expected to adopt the Australian lifestyle and that government agencies and employers had not adjusted their structures and services to respond to the needs of new arrivals, especially those from a non-English speaking background.

They came from Egypt where members of the resident Greek, Italian, Maltese, Jewish and Coptic communities were either forced or felt pressured to leave with the rise of Arab nationalism.

Armenians came from many countries, having dispersed from their homeland in Eastern Anatolia following Turkish atrocities during World War I. In the 1950s they came from trading communities in South and South-East Asia after the fall of colonial Empires. In the 1960s they fled from political upheavals in Middle-East countries. They also came from Greece and Cyprus. In 1962-3 the Australian government operated a special assistance scheme for Armenians in Egypt.

'A land of peace and freedom'

In the 1950s and 60s Australia accepted refugees from a number of places, including Italians and Yugoslavs displaced from the Trieste region of northern Italy, Hungarians, White Russians, and Czechs and Slovaks. Most of them had fled communist regimes. The government did not impose work contracts in exchange for resettlement as it had done with Displaced Persons after the war.

When Immigration Minister Athol Townley greeted Hungarian refugees who arrived on the *Aurelia* in February 1957 he said that Australia was a land of peace and freedom. 'Let us keep it that way', he said. 'You are in a new world among friends – leave behind any bitter thoughts and memories you may have of your experiences in Europe. All that we have we will share with you. You will find great opportunities for yourself and your children. Above all, you will be living in a free land among friendly people.'

The Good Neighbour, No 38, March 1957

Looking tired and bewildered after their arrival at Mascot airport in Sydney, these Hungarian refugees were among ten thousand offered sanctuary by Australia. They had fled from Hungary in the aftermath of the communist revolution there in 1956.

Australian Jewish groups organised their own airlifts, although Australian authorities did not discriminate against Jews in their own program, in contrast to limits imposed on Holocaust survivors.

In 1968 and 1969 Australia accepted four and a half thousand Czech and Slovak refugees. They had fled their country as armed forces from communist-dominated Warsaw Pact countries invaded and occupied Czechoslovakia in August 1968.

This family of White Russian refugees from China arrived at Sydney's Mascot airport in July 1965. They were part of a community of Russians who had first fled to China after the communist revolution in Russia in 1917. Then from 1949 they fled from China's communist revolution.

About seven thousand were resettled in Australia, some coming from a small island in the Philippines where they had been relocated in 1949 by the IRO. Others came direct from Harbin, the main White Russian settlement in China. Most were assisted to resettle by the World Council of Churches.

White Australia

Throughout the 1950s and 60s, the White Australia Policy remained a guiding force in determining the make-up of the Australian population.

Although small numbers of non-Europeans and part-Europeans were admitted into Australia, it was only according to exemption categories introduced by government in response to particular cases and situations. This had been the government's practice since 1901. Non-European settlers were not actively recruited.

Above: Most of the Japanese nationals interned in Australia during the war and other Asians granted refuge when Japan invaded their countries were deported under the 1949 *War-time Refugees Removal Act*. But small numbers of people of mixed European and Asian descent, displaced after the fall of colonial Empires in Asia at the end of World War II, were allowed to resettle in Australia. Robert Nicoll, of Anglo-Indian background and a former captain in the British Army in India, was one of the first when he came on the s.s. *Asturias* in 1948. By the 1960s, other Anglo-Indians, Sri Lankan Burghers and Anglo-Burmese had also arrived.

Neng Hwan Wang was based in Australia as a military attache for China during the war. He married Mabel Wing Dann from a prominent Melbourne Chinese family. In 1946 they moved to Shanghai, but with uncertain times looming in China, they returned in 1948. Neng Hwan Wang was permitted entry under an exemption category for Chinese merchants. He anglicised his name and began the successful merchandising chain of David Wang Emporium. David also made a lifetime commitment to serving the City of Melbourne.

In 1952 the Menzies government introduced temporary residence permits to overcome problems associated with a blanket ban on non-European arrivals.

Temporary residence permits allowed Australian servicemen who had been stationed in Japan with the occupying forces, to bring their Japanese war brides into Australia. Initially the Australian government had banned their entry.

In 1950 Kumi Fuzioka, dressed in a traditional wedding kimono, married Maxwell Barnes. She had met him while she was working in a souvenir shop. She and Maxwell sailed for Australia with other couples and children in 1953. In all, two hundred war brides arrived. Kumi and Maxwell settled down to family life in Tasmania.

In the late 1960s, Australia accepted settlers from Mauritius, an Indian Ocean island under the jurisdiction of the United Kingdom. Moves towards independence had made life uncertain there. Most settlers were European or part-European and arrived as unassisted immigrants. Like Jeannette Antoinette, seen here with her parents at Mauritius airport in 1968, most had a French-Mauritian background, with French or Creole as their first language. Jeannette's brothers were already in Australia and later her parents joined her.

The Australian government made small but significant changes to the White Australia Policy during the 1950s. In 1956 non-European residents were allowed to apply for citizenship. In the 1958 *Migration Act* the infamous Dictation Test was abolished as a method for excluding non-European arrivals. The government used other entry controls.

In the 1960s, public opinion, particularly in universities, began to openly criticise Australia's restrictive immigration policies.

It was also becoming harder to justify the White Australia Policy on the international front. With changing public opinion at home, the government reassessed its restrictive policy and in a cautious move in 1966 allowed non-Europeans with professional and academic qualifications in demand in Australia to apply for entry.

In universities Australians came into contact with non-European students from Africa, Asia and the Pacific, studying in Australia under the 1950 Colombo Plan. Overseas students, such as members of this class in the medical school at Monash University in 1963, defied the stereotype of Asians as the 'Yellow Peril'.

'Make us one people'

In the 1960s Commonwealth and State governments also reassessed policies which discriminated against Indigenous Australians.

In the 1950s and 60s Aboriginal and Torres Strait Islander activists, such as Faith Bandler and Charles Perkins, and their supporters in the wider Australian community, campaigned for an end to racist state laws that oppressed Indigenous Australians. They called for a referendum to change the 1901 Federal Constitution in order to give the Commonwealth power to legislate for Indigenous Australians and to include them in the census of the population.

In 1967 Faith Bandler (right) held up a protest poster demanding that all Australians be counted together as 'One People'. Ironically,

in the 1890s 'One People, One Destiny' had been the slogan for a Federation which excluded Indigenous Australians and non-European settlers.

In 1967 the Australian people overwhelmingly voted yes in a referendum to amend the constitution. This political change, however, did not alter the fact that most Indigenous Australians continued to live in poverty and faced racism in their daily lives. They continued their campaign for equality of access to funding for health, housing, education and training for employment.

'Immigration builds a nation'

Skilled and unskilled, in trades and in the professions, in factories, on farms and in business, immigrants played their part in creating economic development, economic diversity and national prosperity.

The two year contract

For two years after their arrival, Displaced Persons were required to work on construction projects, for government utilities and in factories, often in remote and harsh locations.

Displaced Persons planted forestry trees and worked in timber mills.

They worked on the Hydro-Electric Scheme at Butler's Gorge in Tasmania. Many were Polish ex-servicemen from the British armed forces. At the end of the war, the British government negotiated their settlement in Australia under the same deal offered to Displaced Persons in European refugee camps. Over three hundred soldiers were demobilised in Australia in July 1947 and sent to Butler's Gorge.

'We had to do dirty jobs which most Australians wouldn't touch'.

'I think Australia made a huge mistake. There were a great many doctors and engineers and they had to work as labourers. It was a waste of professional skills and talents.'

'I think the contract was a good thing. It gave people a start.'

Perspectives on the contract from former DPs, Migration Museum oral history interviews, 1994

Displaced Persons constructed roads and railway lines. They laid sewers and pipes.

Right: Many of the men lived in tents with only basic facilities during their contract. Such living conditions were commonly provided for all workers, Australian and overseas-born, as they toiled on large development projects, especially in isolated areas.

'The tents had dirt floors. Each man was given a bag of straw and a cover. It amazed us that we had come 17 000 kilometres across the world and the same type of bedding was used in the camps'. Former DP

Left: Others worked in the hostels as cleaners, office and maintenance staff, or in the kitchens and hospital.

They picked the grape harvest, worked in factories, or as cleaners in hospitals.

On completion of their contract, many Displaced Persons moved into other more skilled occupations. Some opened small businesses. A few went on to become highly successful, wealthy and influential businessmen.

Andreas Dezsery, a political scientist and jounalist in Hungary before the war, opened his New Australian Cleaning Company and also started a publishing firm.

Polish-born Eudoxia Rakowski and her husband opened a delicatessen in Port Adelaide.

Many who worked for government utilities, such as the railways, stayed on in the same work often until retirement, happy with the job security.

Others felt bitter that their professional qualifications were not accepted in Australia, especially when family and financial commitments made studying and retraining difficult.

For some the only choice was part-time study over many years. In 1962, fourteen years after their arrival, three former Displaced Persons, originally from Estonia, posed for a graduation photograph at the Australian National University in Canberra. Ingomar Netliv (left) worked for the Bureau of Census and Statistics, and Kristof Kalma and Paul Magi worked for CSIRO.

'Playing their part': The Snowy Mountains Scheme

The Snowy Mountains Scheme symbolised the pivotal role of immigrants in Australia's post-war development.

This huge engineering and construction project commenced in 1949. It involved diverting the waters of the Snowy and Tumut Rivers in the Great Dividing Range westward onto the dry inland plains for irrigation. As the water flowed down through tunnels and dams its energy was harnessed to generate electricity for New South Wales and Victoria.

Migrant labour made this project achievable. Displaced Persons worked there alongside immigrants from Italy, Greece, Yugoslavia, Norway, West Germany, Austria, Britain and many other lands. Australian-born workers also worked for the various construction and engineering firms. Isolated from the rest of Australia, the workers, regardless of their backgrounds, developed a close camaraderie as they worked together and rested in the huts and canteens.

Most worked in back-breaking dangerous jobs. In the push to complete the project on time, well over a hundred workers lost their lives in horrific accidents in rockfalls and in premature explosions, in tunnelling accidents and on the icy roads. Many others were injured.

For sixteen years, from 1950, Russian Displaced Person, Kiril Makeyev worked as a surveying engineer on the project. The Snowy Mountains Scheme provided some Displaced Persons with an opportunity to work in skilled areas with responsibilities beyond the labouring jobs stipulated in their two-year contract.

The Makeyev family lived in the Snowy Mountains township of Jindabyne. The townships close to the project had residents drawn from many countries. It was a hard life for wives and children in the remote mountain country. Here in 1955 Kiril's son Alexander posed with his first Australian-made snowman.

Filling the gaps

As Displaced Persons finished their two-year contracts and moved on to other jobs, some of the government utilities and construction projects were left critically short of labour. In 1951 the Australian government devised a scheme to recruit over 2000 German nationals. Until this time, these former enemies were not considered suitable immigrants.

Over six hundred went to the Snowy Mountains Scheme. In March 1967 this photograph appeared in *The Good Neighbour* bulletin. A group of German-born Canberra residents was planning a reunion. Committee member, Otto Lauer, said: 'I intended to go straight back to Germany after finishing my two-year contract. But here I still am after sixteen years and I think many of the others would be the same'.

'This is a photograph of my father, Joachim Hasse (right), with friends in Adelaide (SA) in December 1951. He had been working in Berlin in a gang clearing rubble caused by the bombing raids during the war. He heard that the South Australian Railways were seeking young men. There was nothing to keep him in Berlin as he had lost most of his family in the war. He saw it as a chance to start anew. Dad stayed with the railways, although he had trained as a chemist before the war. But here he had to go back to study if he wanted to be a chemist again. But with a young family he needed work. Other Germans went into business or opened restaurants. Some went to Holdens, or like Dad, stayed in the railways.' Peter Hasse, 1999.

Workers of all kinds

Australia's priority after the war was workers for its coal and steel industries. Migrants poured in to fill the job vacancies at places such as Port Kembla (NSW) shown here in 1955.

With a steady supply of steel, other projects could proceed. Immigrants found skilled and unskilled work on the railways and in shipyards, on sewerage projects and in dam and bridge construction. They built roads, houses and offices, schools and shops in the rapidly expanding suburbs.

The Changing Face of Australia

Many of the workers who came out as assisted immigrants lived in hostels, provided by the government or employers close to large work sites, until savings and circumstances gave them the opportunity to move out. The kitchen staff at Villawood Hostel in Sydney in 1957 had the huge daily task of preparing cut lunches for resident workers. Note the selection and number of sandwiches on the order board.

In the 1950s and 60s, many Australians could afford to buy, especially with readily available credit, a car, a fridge, a washing machine, a lawn mower, a television, a vacuum cleaner. New settlers found work on assembly lines making these and other consumer goods.

Just over half of the four and a half thousand workers at the Ford car plant in Geelong (Vic), shown here in 1955 at the end of a working day, were migrants.

Five fitters lined up for a photograph at Tasmania's aluminium plant at Bell Bay in 1958. Only two were Australian-born. The other three had recently arrived from Scotland. The Department of Immigration was keen to promote the notion that workers, regardless of their place of origin, worked in harmony in Australia.

New settlers found work in a diverse range of occupations and businesses beyond the major manufacturing and construction industries. The Department of Immigration extensively publicised the range of options and career opportunities open to newcomers.

By 1966 Paul Kahl (left) and partner Frank Hadley, originally from California (USA), were among more than a hundred Americans who pioneered cotton production in the sheep grazing district of Wee Waa (NSW).

In 1966, Romano Rubichi, a graduate from Modena Teachers College in Italy, took up teaching in the South Australian Education Department. After learning English, he went on to make it one of his teaching subjects.

After arriving in 1963, Felicity Rhodes from Warwickshire, England, opened a fashion boutique in Geraldton (WA), making extensive use of British pop culture which was all the rage in Australia at the time.

Dutch migrant, Fred Witsenhuysen, formerly a cadet journalist in The Hague, worked first on newspapers in Tasmania and Western Australia, eventually becoming a sub-editor of *The News* in Adelaide.

In 1957 Polish-born Stanislaw Perejmibia identified in the photographic caption only as a 'New Australian', became the first New Australian lad to take the Postal Clerks training course in Perth (WA).

Dutch-born doctor Arien van de Meene was photographed examining 'a brand new Australian' in the maternity section of the Ipswich (Qld) General Hospital for an article in *The Good Neighbour* in 1969. The report emphasised how 'a young Dutchman… soon overcame language difficulties to become a brilliant student and gain a medical degree'.

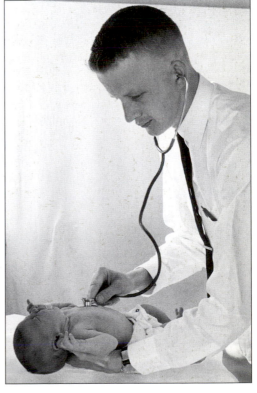

'Great contribution'

'I believe that in the future, European settlers will make a great contribution to Australian art, education, politics, science and industry. The ultimate result will be the creation of a highly individual, unique Australian nation. A combination of the best British and European qualities will so elevate Australia that she will be one of the really great powers of the world in the next century.'

Minister for Immigration, Mr AR Downer, quoted in *The Good Neighbour*, No 107, December 1962.

Seasonal work on the land gave many new arrivals
their start in Australia.

Like many young men in decades past, these
Italian men, fresh off the *Flaminia* in 1955,
were headed for Queensland's cane fields
after their customs checks. Although cane
cutting was backbreaking work, the pay was
good, with skilled cutters earning up to forty
pounds a week during the six months of the
cutting season.

Seasonal fruit and vegetable pickers often
worked long hours and lived in makeshift
accommodation. Italian arrival Antonio
Congedi lived in a tin shed adjoining a stable
when he got his first job on a fruit block at
Redcliffs (Vic) in 1957. Although tin huts were
commonly used to house workers in the
Riverland, Antonio found conditions
unbearable. It was hot, dusty and rain leaked
in. He took a photograph to remember it by.

At the same time Aboriginal stockmen, who had long been the backbone of the outback pastoral industry, endured a far greater level of exploitation in the workforce. They were poorly paid or only in kind. In the 1960s stockmen, especially in the Northern Territory, took successful action to change this situation. In 1966 new Commonwealth legislation gave them equal wages and award conditions.

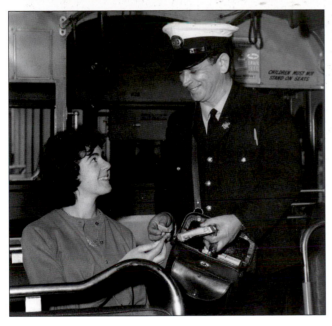

When Maltese settler, Amabile Mifsud, conductor, was pictured at work for the Metropolitan Tramways Trust in Adelaide (SA) in 1966, the MTT's General Manager, FR Harris, was quoted as saying: 'We have always found Maltese people to be competent and happy workers… we are glad to have them'. Maltese settlers, along with other southern Europeans, were not always made to feel this welcome, but the 1950s and 60s were a time of full employment and immigrants were not perceived as a threat to the livelihoods of Australian workers.

Some new arrivals were attracted to the armed forces as a career. Sergeant Geoff Wilson, formerly in the Royal Dragoon Guards in Scotland, was immediately eligible to join the Australian Army because of his British citizenship. He joined the First Armoured Regiment at Puckapunyal (Vic) in the mid 1960s. Non-British European settlers had to take up Australian citizenship before they could join.

In the 1950s, however, national service, served within Australia, was compulsory for all eligible young men. Then in 1967, when conscription was introduced during the Viet Nam conflict, registration for national service overseas became compulsory for all twenty-year-old men, regardless of place of birth or nationality. A ballot based on birth dates then conscripted some of them for service in Viet Nam. Three months after entering national service, non-British settlers could apply for Australian citizenship.

'Happy workers'

The Australian government was particularly keen to promote the notion that migrant workers were satisfied in their jobs in Australia.

When John Glover, precision toolmaker originally from Scotland, was photographed in Newcastle in 1954 at Joseph Sankey & Son, he said he had no complaints about the working conditions, the pay or the country. John was in the fortunate position of having his qualifications readily recognised in Australia. Skilled migrants sometimes experienced difficulties in getting their qualifications and skills recognised.

Migrant workers were involved in building some of Australia's significant public buildings.

More than sixty per cent of the labourers, carpenters and highly skilled craftsmen employed to build the Opera House in Sydney in the 1960s were settlers from Europe.

Women in the workforce

The emphasis on manpower for the steel, construction and building industries may suggest that women weren't in the picture. Migrant and Australian women, single and married, were a significant presence in the workforce.

Many others stayed at home to look after the 'baby boomers'. Migrant mothers of a non-English speaking background were often isolated in their suburban homes. Unlike their husbands who could more easily learn on the job, women struggled to learn English. Their school-aged children became their teachers and intermediaries with the wider community.

Women at this time took on jobs as cleaners, typists, ledger machinists, clerks, stenographers, nurses and teachers. They worked on assembly lines and in food processing factories. But they did not have equal pay or the same working conditions and job security as men. They often had to resign on marrying. Women in the professions, such as architecture, medicine and engineering were rare.

The Department of Immigration employed women in the Social Welfare Section and as shipboard information officers. Senior positions, including migration officers, tended to be filled by men. English-born Mollie Smart worked on the *Fairsea*. She had lived in Australia for seven years before World War II, and returned to England where she became secretary of the Birmingham British-Australian Cobbers' Club. The official caption for this photograph says that after she migrated to Australia in 1959 she 'made British migration to Australia her main interest in life'.

Running a business

For many immigrants, especially those from a non-English speaking background, running a small business or property was a step to economic independence and success in Australia.

Many settlers opened businesses associated with growing or selling food. It didn't require a lot of English or much money to make a start. Often it was possible to live on the premises to reduce costs. The extended family worked hard over long hours as an economic unit.

When Italian Gemilio Sagazio was photographed in Darwin in 1967 he had his own concreting business. He was typical of many immigrants who moved from unskilled work on the land and in factories in the first years after arrival to operating a successful business. Gemilio arrived in Australia in 1956, laying railway sleepers in outback New South Wales, cutting cane in Queensland and clearing scrub for farmland in Victoria.

In the 1950s, the Aloisi family opened a continental delicatessen in Dee Why (NSW). They had arrived earlier in Australia but opened the business when they saw a growing number of new European settlers moving into their area.

Right: After arriving in 1950 and working in various jobs in Sydney and Melbourne, Giuseppe Giudice (far right) became a butcher in North Melbourne, working at Young's Butcher Emporium.

French cousins from Marseilles, Andre Perez and Pierre Falco, photographed in their Sydney restaurant in 1970, were like many other European settlers who opened up cafes and restaurants across Australia. Among their customers were young Australians who, after travelling overseas, returned willing to try new tastes.

'I insist that you must at least consider that more and more there are new people coming to this state, to this city, and I am offering you to be the first to satisfy the new customers with a cake which will be very much in demand.'

With these words in 1952, Kazmer Ujvari convinced an Adelaide retail store to sell his continental-style cakes.

Hungarian-born Kazzy was then twenty-four, a refugee from war-torn Europe. No money and no connections, just his trade as a pastrycook and plenty of determination.

'When I established Budapest Cakes it didn't make any difference that I was a migrant. I was lucky that my trade was recognised and people liked my product, especially the sponge cakes filled with butter cream.'

Other European settlers, especially from southern Europe, applied their knowledge of subsistence farming practised in their villages back home to commercial fruit and vegetable production in Australia.

This is a photograph taken in Werribee (Vic) in the 1930s of cauliflowers harvested by the Sicilian-born Acciarito family for sale in the markets in nearby Melbourne.

1950s arrivals were often attracted to areas such as Werribee and Queensland's Stanthorpe district which had been settled in earlier decades, often by older relatives and former village neighbours. These new arrivals then further consolidated and expanded agricultural production across Australia. The Stanthorpe district became renowned as one of the most prolific fruit-growing areas in Australia.

By 1969 Angelo Masiello, originally coming from Italy in 1952, had become a successful crayfisherman at Geraldton (WA). Many Italian, Croatian and Greek settlers applied their knowledge of the sea to expanding Australia's diverse fishing and boat-building industries. They worked as fishermen, fleet operators, boat-builders, suppliers, fish processors and vendors.

Not all small businesses were associated with food.

Poppy Sidiropoulos obtained a hairdressing diploma and then opened her own salon in her Melbourne home in 1957. The sign advertising her business was an early example of bilingual advertising more common in later decades.

First Spinelli Factory
1962

In the early 1960s Elena and Sante Spinelli launched a highly successful knitting factory in Adelaide, using fine grade Merino wool processed in their former homeland, Italy, to create exquisite fashion garments.

THE CHANGING FACE OF AUSTRALIA

Immigrants also brought specialist skills to Australia.

Greek sponge-fishers from the island of Kalymnos were specially recruited in 1954 for their diving skills in an effort to revive Australia's pearling industry.

But at the same time, another Greek arrival, who had settled in the Top End in 1919, used his business skills to take the pearling industry in a new direction. Before the war the emphasis was on harvesting mother-of-pearl for use in buttons and cutlery. Nicholas Paspaley began to experiment in cultivating pearls. Here he is shown in the 1950s working with a Japanese technician. His son, also Nicholas, further refined pearl cultivation methods and by the late 1990s Paspaley pearls had become renowned across the world for their exceptional quality and beauty.

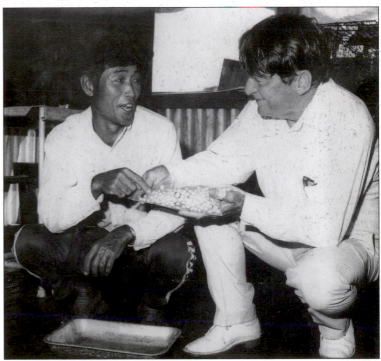

Dutch-born craftsman, Andres de Jager, came from the Netherlands in 1952 and by 1962 had an Australia-wide reputation for the classical guitars and other musical instruments he made in his Perth (WA) shop. He also repaired instruments for the Western Australian Symphony Orchestra.

In the early 1950s Aldo Rossi brought centuries of Italian tradition and skill in mosaic work to bear as he constructed the mosaic mural created by Australian artist Napier Waller for the Hall of Memories at the Australian War Memorial in Canberra (ACT). A Melbourne firm, De Marco Brothers, brought Aldo out from Italy specifically for the huge job which involved over six million mosaic pieces.

Making Australia home

For immigrants and especially refugees, regardless of country of origin or year of arrival, setting up house was a priority.

The publicity said that you could own your own home in Australia. It was not easy, though. In the first years after the war, houses and building materials were in short supply and many new assisted arrivals found themselves living in hostel accommodation for months and years.

Often both parents worked hard in more than one job to achieve their dream of owning their own home.

With the large influx of immigrants in the 1950s, Australians were encouraged to be generous and offer whatever accommodation they had to ease the housing shortage. Bronius (on left, with workmates in June 1950) and Maria Kapociunas, Displaced Persons from Lithuania, rented a backyard shed in suburban Adelaide. Others improvised, using the timber from large crates used for importing cars to construct their homes.

'There was no running water, no electricity. The children slept on the floor. The rain used to come in. I got some kind of infection. The doctor came in with a little candle. He said, Look, you can't live like his.'
Maria Kapociunas

For others, like the Simson family from England who settled in Adelaide and began to construct their house in 1955, it was months of do-it-yourself house construction on weekends or after work.

These British settlers in Sydney in 1958 were typical of many who formed or joined co-operative societies to help each other purchase building materials and provide skills and labour.

This photograph, captioned *An Immigrant's view of Broadmeadows (Melbourne) 1950s*, captures the experience of many settlers who bought land in new housing developments on the fringes of the suburbs. Without nearby shops, roads, footpaths and trees, with dust in summer and mud in winter, life was stark and lonely. It was worlds away from the close-knit European and British village and city life.

Some post-war arrivals settled in older inner city suburbs or rural communities established by earlier generations of immigrants. There they rekindled extended family and village ties. These communities rarely became the closed enclaves that critics of the government's post-war immigration program predicted. Like other Australians, settlers were highly mobile. Intermarriage was common and the younger generation moved on to other suburbs and cities.

State governments offered subsidised rental housing to encourage immigrants to their states. The South Australian government planned a new satellite city, north of Adelaide, to attract British immigrants. The city of Elizabeth, named after Queen Elizabeth II, was built from the late 1950s following the latest in British urban design. The streets, hotels and public areas were given English names to create an illusion of familiarity for new British arrivals.

First things

Official government photographs mostly recorded immigrants making a contribution in the public arena. Photographs taken by refugees and immigrants themselves record more personal milestones. These significant moments signalled a hope that the future would be better than the past.

Greta Deckys, a former Displaced Person from Lithuania, posed beside the first washing machine she purchased in Australia, after saving hard to pay cash for it.

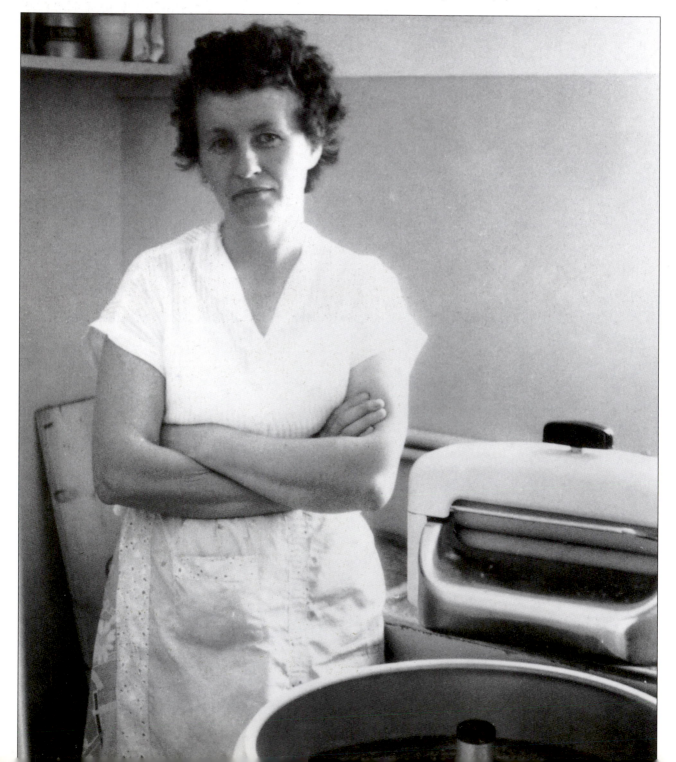

Three women who arrived in Australia as Displaced Persons, proudly held their first Australian-born babies, all born at Woodside hostel (SA) in early 1950.

Ukrainian DP, Lea Sziller, was thrilled with the first dress she purchased after arriving in Australia in 1949. Back in the refugee camps in Germany and even further back to the war, new clothes and dress fabrics were an unobtainable luxury.

Alfredo Floramo, a Displaced Person from Italy, was proud of his first bicycle, even if he had only the desert to ride in after being sent to the railway fettlers' camp at Rawlinna (WA) in 1951 as part of his two-year work contract.

Happy but disliked

When settlers began to acquire the trappings of success, some encountered resentment and jealousy, suggesting that many Australians believed that immigrants belonged, and should stay, at the bottom of the socio-economic ladder. A letter in *The Good Neighbour* bulletin from Hobart (Tas) in the 1960s expressed this problem:

'Sir, I have been in Australia for fifteen years, having migrated from Greece in 1953. It took me four or five years to find out how Australians like people to live in this country. I am happy in this country because I am an Australian now. But in the past few years Australians have seemed to dislike us – because we have a car, we have a home, we have a job, and so on. Jealousy is a bad sickness for anyone to have. We cannot be like a happy family if they talk to us in this way.'

In 1957 in Perth (WA) Polish DP, Franciszek Samojlowicz posed with his son in front of his first Holden car.

New Australians and Good Neighbours

Immigrants were called 'New Australians', a term which carried the expectation that they would adopt Australian ways as quickly as possible. 'Old' Australians were, at the same time, encouraged to be 'good neighbours' and help new arrivals blend in.

At the heart of this policy of assimilation was the fear that European settlers would form enclaves, decline to contribute to the wider community, and threaten Australia's social cohesion.

The Australian government, through its monthly bulletin, *The Good Neighbour*, gave new arrivals plenty of advice on adopting the Australian way of doing things. Articles reassured them that Australia's policemen were friendly, admonished them for carrying knives which no one in Australia needed to do, instructed them on how to make a sandwich and warned them of the dangers of the surf and the bushfire.

Common ground

Immigrants shared, and continue to share, many values in common with Australians.

Australians participated with overwhelming enthusiasm in celebrations for the coronation of Queen Elizabeth II in 1953 and her visit to Australia in 1954. These two occasions became photo opportunities for the Department of Immigration to show new European settlers reassuringly expressing their loyalty to the Queen. 'New Australians' were encouraged to add a 'touch of colour' by wearing their national costumes wherever the Queen appeared.

Immigrants who had served on the Allies' side during World War II participated in Australia's day of remembrance, Anzac Day. Poles who marched down Adelaide's King William Street in 1961 were but one group. Ex-servicemen and women from Britain, Greece, Malta, Serbia, New Zealand, the United States of America, Canada, the Netherlands and France marched alongside Australian comrades-in-arms. The war, which brought so many to Australia, was also a common bond. In later decades, they would be joined by ex-servicemen from other wars, including the Vietnam conflict of the late 1960s and early 1970s.

THE CHANGING FACE OF AUSTRALIA

New arrivals who excelled at sport, be it swimming or football or any other game, found that it was a ready way to gain nation-wide acceptance in Australia. Swimming champions, twins John and Ilsa Konrads, from Latvia, shown here with coach Don Talbot, were among sixteen 'New Australians' who were part of the 1960 team heading for the Olympic Games in Rome.

When White Russian beauty, Tania Verstak, who had arrived as a refugee from China in 1951, was crowned 'Miss Australia of 1961', she was, according to Immigration Minister, Alexander Downer, 'the ultimate demonstration… of the way in which our new settlers have entered the hearts and lives of the Australian people'. Many other immigrants, however, faced bigotry and discrimination in their daily lives and did not always feel welcomed in Australia. Tania publicly expressed the hope that she would be able to bring new and old Australians closer together through her position as Miss Australia.

Families often took their own personal photographs of their adaptation to the Australian lifestyle. The Daws family, from England, photographed son Christopher swimming at Garratt Road Bridge in January 1969 in Belmont, Perth (WA), because it was 'an unknown delight before migrating from England'.

And in 1961 German settlers, Helene and Josef Sandl and their friends, did the same as many other Australian families and their visitors on hot summer evenings. They took the television, Australia's new cultural obsession, outside to the backyard where it was cooler. What were they watching? A program from America perhaps?

The Department of Immigration took many photographs to demonstrate the ease and enthusiasm with which immigrants took up Australian pastimes. This Dutch family, formerly from The Hague and living in a Sydney beachside suburb, were chosen to show how they enjoyed a day at the beach, just like any Australian family, in the summer of 1965.

Dressing up

From the time of the first arrivals in 1947, 'New Australians' were frequently invited to dance, sing and play music in national costume at civic celebrations and events, at concerts and arts festivals around Australia. It was one way for new arrivals to share their cultural traditions and break down barriers in Australian society. Many Australians were entranced by the 'exotic' performances, but formed a perception that folk arts and crafts were all that European settlers had to offer to Australian performing and visual arts. In reality, overseas-born settlers made diverse and significant contributions to all forms of arts and cultural activities.

In 1951 Ukrainian dancers appeared at a Highland gathering at Manuka Oval in Canberra.

New settlers may well have been expected to assimilate into Australian society, but it was naïve to expect them to discard the cultural practices that gave meaning to their lives as if it were as easy as taking off a coat on a hot day. And of course, it didn't happen like that.

One of Estonian-born Ene-Mai Reinpuu's cherished photographs shows an Estonian folk group posing in Bonegilla hostel in 1949 for a photograph before leaving to perform at a concert. In a democratic and free Australia, Displaced Persons were able to cherish and nurture their cultural traditions that were suppressed in their former homelands by Soviet communism.

THE CHANGING FACE OF AUSTRALIA

Below: A Lithuanian priest stood with his class after their lessons on Lithuanian language and heritage at Woodside (SA) migrant hostel in the 1950s. This scene was repeated around Australia as Displaced Persons, and other new settlers, sought to give their children knowledge about a former homeland that most would never see.

By the 1970s these informal classes had evolved into an extensive network of 'ethnic' schools involving most settler groups. Differences in language, customs and values between European-born parents and their Australian-born children became an extra element in the usual parent-child friction, especially aggravated by the emerging global youth culture.

Above: Polish Displaced Persons, cherishing Australia's political freedom, organised protest rallies, this one in Tasmania in 1956, to publicly denounce the Soviet oppression of their homeland. A freedom denied their compatriots back home.

New settlers set about re-creating in Australia the tastes and pastimes of former lives in another land, in another time.

In Adelaide in the 1950s, Swiss settler, Max Schleuniger, imported a prefabricated house from his former homeland of Switzerland so that he could have the kind of home he would have lived in back there. The fir tree in the front garden was a further reminder of his homeland.

THE CHANGING FACE OF AUSTRALIA

In the late 1950s, the Chiarolli and Nassig households, originally from Italy, made wine in their backyard. And the Orsetto family killed a pig on their Stanthorpe (Qld) property to make salami, pancetta, cotecchini and pork sausages. It was a day of fun and excitement, eating fresh pork sausages and enjoying a glass or two of homemade wine.

Back in Italy, these were seasonal routines to keep up household food supplies. In Australia the winemaking and pig-killing had also become a way to remember places and faces left behind. The significance of the occasion had been forever changed in the new landscape.

Presto Smallgoods Factory in Leichhardt,
Sydney, was one of many businesses opened
by new settlers to provide familiar continental
smallgoods. With work demands and the
different suburban lifestyle in Australia it was
not always possible to cook, prepare and store
food according to traditional methods.

Many Europeans missed the café culture of Europe. Australia's pubs, a male domain, shocked and dismayed many a new arrival. Australian men crowded into the front bars. Women sat in separate lounges or husbands took them out a shandy while they waited in the car. The swilling of the last beers at six o'clock each evening before the pubs closed seemed the ultimate in uncivilised behaviour. Enterprising settlers established European-style cafes and served espresso coffee, wine and tortes. The Popular Café set up by Hungarian settlers in the 1950s in Mullumbimby (NSW) gave new settlers there some of the tastes and style of home. It wasn't long before Australians ventured in.

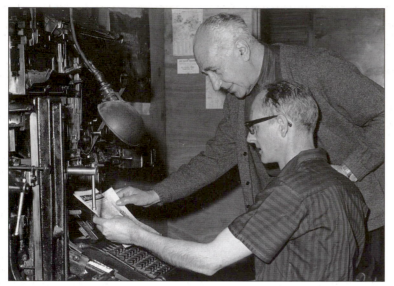

In post-war Australia community language newspapers gave new settlers a chance to keep up with world and local Australian events in their own language. When Dr Mark Siegelberg (top) founded the German language paper *Neue Welt* (*New World*) he believed it would play a vital role in helping new German settlers successfully adjust to life in Australia and in helping children retain a knowledge of their parents' language.

European arrivals brought with them a passion for the game of soccer. Across Australia, the various national groups established teams and competitions. Loyalty to the club became synonymous with loyalty to one's origins, with many teams using colours or emblems of the old homeland.

Some arrivals began to play Australian Rules football, but generally taking up Aussie Rules was left to the sons some years further on. Not many 'old' Australians changed from football to soccer, with the result that soccer was sidelined as an 'ethnic' game and struggled to catch the attention of Australian sports-writers. New European settlers boosted participation and skill levels in a diverse range of sports, including fencing, table tennis, athletics and basketball.

For Angelo Aslanidis the significance of this
1956 photograph of he and fellow young
Greek workmates employed by the Tasmanian
Hydro-Electric Commission was that they were
drinking beer, not ouzo. They were
becoming Australian.

Join the club

New settlers established clubs and associations. Many evolved from informal gatherings in people's homes to purpose-built clubrooms with entertaining, performance, sporting and kitchen facilities. Others joined clubs started decades earlier by previous generations of immigrants, often reigniting community spirit that had declined due to an ageing and diminishing membership. Still others declined to join any clubs at all, preferring to blend in to the wider community or steer clear of what they perceived as group rivalries and internal politics.

By the end of the 1960s clubs established by new settlers had extended and enhanced Australia's diverse and vibrant community life, and assisted many arrivals to adjust to life in a new homeland.

Clubs provided a place where new settlers could get together with people of the same background, language and shared history. They gave people a sense of belonging in a country that didn't always make them feel welcome. These gatherings, ranging from sporting events, to festivals, picnics and the celebration of national days, reminded them of who they were and where they came from. Here Finns from around Australia gathered for the Finnish National Festival at Ainslie Oval in Canberra (ACT) in 1965.

Above: In 1965, at the British Women's Club in Adelaide women shared not only the common experience of being an immigrant, but also a cup of coffee, a game of cards, an outing, helping other new arrivals, and knitting.

Right: Clubrooms became venues for dances, music and theatre performances. For members of Sydney's Romanian community there was the joy of having a place to perform their national dance, the Hora.

When immigrants settle in a new land they need to find new reference points for determining their position within the community. In Australia, the rise of clubs based on country or region of origin gave new arrivals a means of gaining positions of respect and influence within their communities and the wider Australian society. Here the 1953 committee members of Sydney's Estonian Club posed for a formal photograph.

Below: In 1964 the first delegation of Lebanese left Sydney to attend a world conference of Lebanese emigrants in London. In the 1950s and 60s clubs became part of state, national and international networks.

Weekends became an important time for immigrant families, as a break from the effort it took to make their new life in Australia a success. In parks and on beaches families and close friends gathered for picnics. George Donikian remembered the picnics his family and friends enjoyed in Lane Cove National Park and at Nielson Park at Vaucluse in Sydney (NSW) in the 1950s: 'The picnics were a welcome break for my father and the other men from working hard during the week. The women would prepare food galore. We'd cook on a spit. It was a chance to relax, enjoy each other's company, laugh and embrace our Greek culture and language'. George also fondly recalled that Nielson Park was nicknamed 'Dagoes Paradise' because of its popularity as a picnic and swimming spot with new settlers.

Rites and rituals

European immigrants in the 1950s and 60s diversified religious observance, architecture and education in Australia. Established Australian churches and 'New' Australians encountered differences in beliefs, rituals, celebrations and attitudes.

It was important to have a place to gather for worship and prayer. When post-war European arrivals of the Lutheran faith wanted to establish a parish church in Ottoway, an Adelaide suburb in the early 1950s, they converted a war-time Nissen hut into a church by adding a tower.

Italian settlers brought with them their festivals honouring the patron saint of the village back home. It was often some years before the community had the time, savings and resources to organise a procession and all of the associated festive activities. In the first years, or even decades, after arrival, there were other priorities.

In this 1970 photograph, the Italian population in Stanthorpe, a fruit-growing district in Queensland, was celebrating the annual Feast of St Joseph the Worker. In the centre is the statue of the saint. Usually, statues of the patron saints were brought out from Italy after fundraising efforts to cover the costs. The statue was kept in a special alcove within the local church during the year.

The arrival of large numbers of European Catholics had a significant impact on the Irish-Catholic Church in Australia. In particular, small parish schools struggled to cope with the huge influx of Australian and European 'baby-boomers'. Class sizes swelled. The Catholic school system expanded rapidly across Australia and forced to a head the long-standing issue of State Aid for independent, church-run schools.

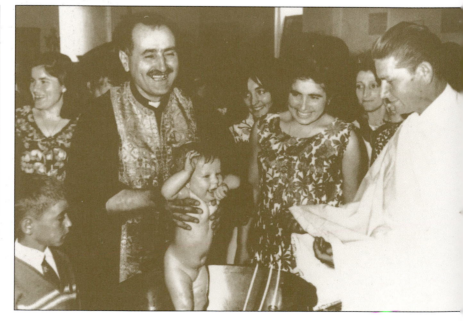

Within the churches, people marked their journey through time. In rites of passage, they married, and introduced their children through baptism and other rituals to the faith that was a part of their cultural heritage.

Not just a quaint, exotic hobby

A New Australian Festival in Canberra in 1949 gave European arrivals a chance to display their arts and crafts. The motifs, designs, textures and colours had meanings immersed in the history, landscapes and stories of their homelands. Methods of weaving, carving and needlework had been passed down from generation to generation. There was now a sense of obligation to keep alive in their new country the traditions and the skills that were suppressed by communist authorities back home. At the same time, many artists and craft workers incorporated new motifs and developed new techniques inspired by the colours, shapes and textures of the Australian landscape.

Migrants for mates

The Australian government encouraged Australians to welcome new settlers into their midst. Joining the Good Neighbour Movement, a nation-wide organisation founded in 1949, was the most popular way that Australians offered their time and energy to assist in the effort to assimilate huge numbers of new immigrants into the Australian way of life.

As volunteers in the Good Neighbour Movement, thousands of Australians offered the hand of friendship to new settlers and introduced them to the way things were done in Australia. Initially most efforts were directed to welcoming British settlers. By the 1960s more overseas-born residents, such as Lily Cvejic, had joined the movement and extended assistance to arrivals from non-English speaking backgrounds. Here she is pictured talking to Yugoslav settlers in the industrial town of Wundowie (WA) in 1968. The onus remained, however, on the new arrival to adjust and fit in.

The reality, however, was that most new arrivals from a non-English speaking background turned for assistance to their own clubs and networks. Clubs began to provide welfare assistance, especially for their ageing members. When the Russian Relief Association opened St Sergius's Home for the Aged in Cabramatta, Sydney, in the 1960s, this woman was able to enjoy the comfort and security of a culturally familiar environment, although unable to remain within her extended family. Australia was a different place demanding new responses.

None of that 'foreign gabble' here!

The Australian government wanted all new settlers to speak English.

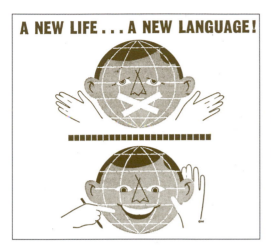

New arrivals attended English classes at Northam camp in Western Australia in 1950. This lesson was one of thousands the Australian government provided free in hostels and schools, by correspondence and on the radio and then television to encourage new settlers to learn English as the first and most important step to blending in. From these tentative beginnings which often relied on volunteer tutors evolved an extensive national system for teaching English to Australia's new arrivals.

Many new arrivals also felt the pressure to convert their European names to a more easily-pronounced Anglo-Celtic version. In the late 1960s, when Netherlands-born Berta van Weely became a television personality in Brisbane she changed her name to Sherry Wheeler.

In reality, this emphasis on speaking English created an atmosphere of intolerance for languages other than English.

'If you were talking on the bus in Polish, people would say, 'This is Australia. Speak Australian or get out'. It wasn't pleasant.'

Former DP in Migration Museum interview, 1994.

'Your share in Australia'

The Australian government encouraged all new settlers to take out Australian citizenship.

citizenship
is your share in Australia

Australia invites migrants who have lived here for 4½ years to apply for Australian citizenship by naturalization. Full details and application forms are available from Department of Immigration offices in capital cities, or branches of the Good Neighbour Movement

The Australian government believed that the numbers of settlers taking up citizenship indicated the success of the immigration program. Each person in the group taking their oath of allegiance at Melbourne Town Hall in 1955 probably had different and complex reasons for taking out citizenship. It was ultimately an individual choice, based on many factors, including feeling pressure to express loyalty and gratitude to Australia.

Most Displaced Persons took out Australian citizenship as hopes faded for a return to their homelands behind the Iron Curtain. Northern and southern Europeans also embraced Australian citizenship in large numbers. Settlers from Britain had least incentive to become Australian citizens as they were entitled to vote and join the armed forces because of their British citizenship and were able to come and go from Australia on their British passports.

The concept of Australian citizenship was new to Australia. Until the passing of the 1948 *Citizenship Act* all Australians were British subjects. The Australian government introduced formal citizenship ceremonies to highlight its civic importance. The first citizenship ceremony was conducted in Canberra's Albert Hall on Australia Day, 26 January, in 1949. Seven settlers were chosen to represent each state and the Australian Capital Territory. They came from seven different places. Some had arrived in Australia in the early decades of the century. Others were recent arrivals. The Prime Minister, Ben Chifley, symbolically accepted Australian citizenship on behalf of all Australians.

One person who was not allowed to line up at any citizenship ceremony in 1955 was Joseph Tong Way. Remember him with his family in Ballarat in 1900? Here is his photograph on an application to the Department of Immigration in 1948 to renew his temporary residence permit. He had been in Australia since 1893. Ironically, it was the year Joseph died, 1956, that the Australian government lifted its citizenship ban on non-European residents.

NAME WAY Joseph TONG

Address 49 Gipps St East Melbourne

Nationality Chinese

Place of Birth Canton

Date of Birth 12/3/82

Single or Married widower

Occupation retired

Arrived in Australia on 1893

Port of Melb per ?

J. J. Way
SIGNATURE OF HOLDER.

Certificate issued at Melbourne

on 12/2/48

Issued by Sahhner

For COMMONWEALTH MIGRATION OFFICER.

Personal Description :

Height 5 ft. 4 ins

Build medium

Eyes Black Hair Black

Remarks

A Change in Focus

By the 1960s there were contradictory and diverging strands in Australian attitudes towards immigrants.

On the one hand, the policy of assimilation continued to direct government and community attitudes.

On the whole, though, by 1965 there was a diminishing emphasis on pressing new settlers to become Anglo-Celtic Australians.

Below: This group was the Western Australian delegation to the 10th Australian Citizenship Convention, held in 1959 at the Albert Hall in Canberra. They belonged to community organisations, church bodies and service clubs. These annual government-led conventions were held to discuss, at a grass-roots level, how best to absorb new settlers into the community. At first there was much talk about preserving Australia's British heritage and preventing the formation of minority groups. But these delegates to the 1959 convention began to hear and use the word 'integrate' rather than 'assimilate', albeit interchangeably at first. Speakers at this and later conventions reflected a subtle shift in attitudes that acknowledged that 'old' and 'new' Australians were forming together new and diverse ways of being Australian.

Below: In Victoria in 1965 the All Nations Together Society held a quest to find the 'best assimilated family'. Mr and Mrs Wendt, former Lithuanian DPs living in the Melbourne suburb of Noble Park and their three sons won because of their voluntary work for the local school and the boys excelled in a number of sports and at their studies. At the presentation of their prize of a two-week holiday in Queensland by Mr Snedden, Commonwealth Attorney-General (second from right), Mr Wendt declared, 'We will regard it as a challenge, rather than a reward, to do a little bit better. Thank you all for accepting us into your midst'.

The Changing Tastes of A Nation

There was also increasing awareness that the influx of migrants had influenced and changed Australian society.

In 1964 when these sales assistants were photographed by the Department of Immigration in the smallgoods section of Myers store in Melbourne, the purpose was to show how 'the influx of migrants (had) caused an increase in imports of food, clothing and furniture, which is also influencing and changing the tastes of natural-born Australians'.

When does a migrant stop being a migrant? How long should it take him to become a member of the Australian community? Should a migrant be expected to cut himself off completely from the way of life he enjoyed in his former homeland? And what of his children, who are caught between two distinct and different ways of life?…There is no simple answer to any of these questions. Are migrants too rigid in their attitudes towards the Australian way of life? How earnestly are older-established Australians trying to understand the migrants' point of view? Is the Australian community now more receptive to new ways of life? In Australia there is room for individual difference, but understanding is essential to achieve meaningful growth and development.

Editorial address, *The Good Neighbour*, No 184, May 1969

1970s – 1990s

BROADENING THE BASE

From the 1970s the pattern of immigration to Australia changed.

The mass migration program for British and European immigrants which characterised the 1950s and 60s ended. The remnants of the White Australia Policy were abolished and a Universal Migration Policy introduced. Assisted passage schemes ended except for refugees. The number of British and European immigrants declined dramatically and arrivals began to come from countries closer to Australia.

High unemployment and slow economic growth, particularly in the 1980s, eroded political and community support for immigration. Opposing those who believed that a strong immigrant intake created economic growth through demand for goods and services were those who argued that immigrants took jobs from Australians. Environmental lobby groups questioned the ability of the Australian environment to sustain continued population growth. The catchcry 'Populate or Perish' had lost favour.

From the 1970s, immigration to Australia from Germany and the Netherlands and from southern European countries, especially Italy, Greece and Malta, virtually ceased. Britain and Europe prospered and there was less readiness to emigrate. Governments no longer viewed emigration as a solution to unemployment and economic problems.

British immigrants continued to dominate arrivals, but in much smaller numbers. Generally, new settlers were from the professions rather than the unskilled or skilled workers who dominated the intake in the 1950s and 60s. In some years, net migration was very low, with restricted quotas and more Australians moving overseas for work.

The last of the 'ten pound tourists'

These arrivals landing in Melbourne on the *Ellinis* in 1973 were among the last British immigrants assisted to Australia on chartered migrant ships. The ten pound passage scheme ended in 1975.

The end of White Australia

In 1973 the Labor Party government, led by Prime Minister Gough Whitlam, implemented a Universal Migration Policy which stipulated that anyone could apply to migrate to Australia regardless of race, colour, gender, ethnic origin, religion or nationality. Immigration agreements with Britain and European countries were abandoned and the government removed differences in citizenship rights between British and non-British settlers.

This policy did not open up the floodgates. The Whitlam government cut the immigration intake during its years of office because of economic recession. Nor was there an immediate change in the number and location of Australian migration offices around the world. Then from 1979 a points system (NUMAS) for entry qualification restricted the number of successful applicants.

A significant proportion of immigrants began to arrive from countries closer to Australia. Within a decade, over 100 000 settlers had arrived from Asia, Africa and the Pacific.

Source countries have included India, Pakistan, Sri Lanka, South Africa, eastern African countries, Malaysia, Singapore, China, Hong Kong, the Philippines, Fiji and other Pacific Islands, in particular from where there had been a British connection

Arrivals were generally affluent, lived in cities rather than rural areas, were fluent in English, and were university graduates and professionals, such as teachers, doctors and engineers. Some had previously studied at Australian universities. They came from a diversity of religious and ethnic backgrounds. Other family members often joined them in Australia.

Sri-Lankan Param Sothy (right) came to Australia from Britain in 1974 as part of this new trend. Other family members also resettled in Australia direct from Sri Lanka. In 1984 his mother, Rasamuthu Selladuray, joined him in Australia under the Family Migration Program after the Department of Immigration waived objections about her failing eyesight on humanitarian grounds. They settled in Adelaide and were photographed there in 1987.

Skills not people

From the 1970s Australian governments stipulated that potential migrants must have skills or professional expertise required to fill gaps in the Australian work force, or business experience and investment capital that would directly benefit the Australian economy. Family reunion remained the other cornerstone of the migration program. Quotas limited the intake, particularly in years of high unemployment or slow economic growth.

Major construction projects have been a source of employment for skilled and unskilled immigrants throughout the 20th century. Here overseas-born civil engineers found work on the Westgate Bridge project in Melbourne in 1974. The construction of major freeways and the Sydney Olympic facilities dominated projects in the 1990s.

These three teachers appointed to Queanbeyan High School (NSW) were among those recruited in the United States of America and Canada by Australian education departments to fill gaps in teacher numbers in the early 1970s.

Skilled Labour and Business Migration programs specifically targeted particular occupational groups. The incentive, however, to immigrate to Australia, rested on more factors than career and business opportunities. The Australian lifestyle and climate remained significant 'pull' factors in encouraging immigration to Australia.

In 1985 John Boland from Dublin Ireland responded to an Australian government campaign to attract trained chefs. He first worked in Queensland as a chef at the Conrad Hotel (pictured) in Surfers Paradise, then on Hamilton Island. Like many other young single men arriving in Australia, he was prepared to move for job opportunities. On his way to work in Perth (WA), he stopped over in Adelaide (SA). There he found work as catering manager in a boarding school.

Below: In 1988 American horticulturalist, Dr Roger Dutcher, came out under the Business Migration program to work in the field of tissue culture at Calgene Pacific's laboratory.

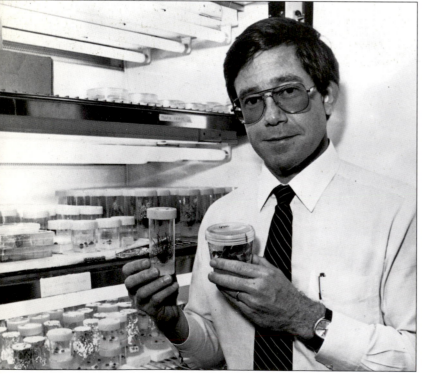

Since the nineteenth century, New Zealanders have crossed the Tasman to work in Australia. Many have stayed only on a short-term basis, working in seasonal jobs. New Zealanders have tended to be young and work as tradesmen and in clerical positions. They have been regarded almost as internal immigrants. In the early years of the twentieth century, most arrivals from New Zealand were Anglo-Celtic. Since the mid 1970s Maoris, the Indigenous people of New Zealand, have also resettled in Australia. Australians have also continued to cross the other way to work in New Zealand. In the 1986 census, over 210 000 Australian residents listed their place of birth as New Zealand.

THE CHANGING FACE OF AUSTRALIA

Hong Kong Chinese families relocated to Australia and other countries such as Canada, in the years leading up to the handing back of Hong Kong in 1997 to China as the 99-year lease signed between Britain and China ended. They came out on business migration programs. They often commuted between Hong Kong and Australia to continue their business activities there, meaning that they were frequently away from their wives and children in Australia.

The Hua family (right) came from China under the Business Migration Program in 1993. At Adelaide International Airport friends already in Adelaide welcomed them. They were among a growing number of Chinese settlers arriving from mainland China, Hong Kong and South-East Asian countries since the late 1960s. Their arrival boosted numbers in the Chinese communities in Australia which had declined since the implementation of the White Australia Policy in 1901 and increased the proportion of Chinese Australians who had been born overseas. Among the new Chinese arrivals were many property developers and entrepreneurs, financiers and bankers who brought a great deal of capital with them to Australia.

Alfredo, Sandra and Daniel: their story

In June 1995 Brazilian couple, Alfredo Goldbach, a psychotherapist, and Sandra de Souza, airline systems analyst with their young son, Daniel, left Rio de Janiero for a new life in Australia.

'We were established and respected professionals in Rio de Janiero. We decided to give ourselves the opportunity to experience life within a culture different than ours. We chose Australia for its interesting cultural and historical position in the world. Sandra had also recently learned that skills like hers were in need'.

Sandra became a systems analyst with Qantas. Alfredo's qualifications were recognised at the end of 1995 and he began work with Jewish Community Services, reflecting his own Jewish background. He also started a part-time practice working in Portuguese, firstly running a group for Portuguese and Spanish speaking men dealing with stress, anxiety and depression at Marrickville Community Health Centre and then practising in association with a Brazilian GP. In his work as a psycho-therapist, Alfredo is 'often faced with helping my clients revisit the pains, losses and gains experienced in their own migration process'.

In this photograph Alfredo and Sandra celebrated Daniel's birthday in their flat at Coogee, Sydney (NSW) with Alfredo's mother, Daisy, who had come on a visit 'to see for herself that the new land was really doing us all the good that the phone calls and the pictures used to tell her it was'.

Many of the photographs Alfredo and Sandra took in the first months after arrival show them in parks, on picnics and at the beach. 'We were a family sticking together to go through the difficult initial impact of changing our references so drastically. Daniel took his first steps and so did we as we learnt about Australians. The beach, being a Brazilian favourite, was something we could certainly identify with.'

'With a well-founded fear'

From the 1970s Australian governments confined assistance programs to refugee groups selected for resettlement in Australia under Australia's obligations to the United Nations. Others, though not strictly refugees, have been accepted on special humanitarian grounds.

In a break from previous practice, Australia also accepted non-European refugees. Most of the refugees arriving in the 1970s and 80s had come from the war-torn Indo-Chinese countries of Vietnam, Cambodia and Laos.

> A refugee is any person who owing to a well-founded fear of being persecuted for reasons of race, religion, nationality, membership of a particular social group or political opinion, is outside the country of his or her nationality and is unable or, owing to such fear, is unwilling to avail himself or herself of the protection of that country.
>
> United Nations Convention, 1951

Among the first refugees to Australia in the 1970s were East Timorese fleeing the Indonesian take-over of the Portuguese-held territory of East Timor. This group arrived by boat in Darwin in August 1975. In all, about 1800 East Timorese were accepted into Australia.

At first, Vietnamese refugees came by boat to Australia's northern shores, the first boats arriving in 1976. They had fled from South Vietnam which, after April 1975, had come under the control of the communist government of North Vietnam. Here in 1977 interpreter My Van Tran assisted Immigration Officer, Ian Marks (both left), to interview refugees in Darwin. The refugees became known in the Australian press as 'boat people'.

Over fifty boats, carrying two thousand refugees, made it to Australia in the late 1970s. They had risked treacherous seas, attacks by pirates, starvation and cramped, primitive conditions on barely seaworthy vessels. It is not known how many people died at sea in the attempt to reach Australia.

Australia had been involved in the Vietnam War since the mid 1960s. Towards the end of the war, in 1974-5, Australia accepted limited numbers of South Vietnamese, namely a few hundred orphaned children adopted by Australians. Other arrivals included families of Vietnamese students resident in Australia, and others associated with Australia's military presence during the war.

It was in camps in Malaysia and in Thailand, crowded with hundreds of thousands of Vietnamese, Cambodian and Laotian men, women and children, where Australian immigration officers processed most refugees from the Indo-China conflicts for eventual acceptance into Australia. To the Australian government, this controlled selection of refugees, with identity and health checks completed prior to arrival, was preferable to random boat arrivals.

Opposite: From 1979 refugees began arriving by air direct from overseas camps to begin a new life in Australia, with nearly 80,000 arriving between 1975 and 1985. The term 'boat people' was often used inaccurately in the press to describe all Vietnamese settlers.

Vietnamese arrivals spent their first months in government hostels. In a break from previous practice, some hostels provided cooking facilities and allowed families to prepare their own meals, acknowledging that roast lamb or chops, the staple fare in hostels throughout the 1950s and 60s, was inappropriate.

Many Vietnamese families were resettled in Australia under the Community Refugee Settlement Scheme (CRSS) which began in 1979. It operated with government support but relied on community volunteers to provide accommodation and assistance to settle in. The Vo family had flown out from a camp in Malaysia in 1980 and was sponsored by Hobart church groups. One of them carried a model of the boat on which they had escaped from Vietnam.

THE CHANGING FACE OF AUSTRALIA

These three Cambodian boys (on right), shown with their Australian sponsors in Canberra in 1983, were among nearly 14 000 Cambodian refugees accepted into Australia between 1975 and 1986. They came to Australia from a Thai refugee camp as 'unaccompanied minors', having lost contact with their families during Pol Pot's Khmer Rouge regime.

Below: Hmong people from the mountains of Laos were also displaced by the Indo-Chinese conflicts. By the mid 1980s about four hundred had arrived in Australia from Thai refugee camps. The Xiong family (below) who arrived in 1988 were helped to settle in to life in Tasmania by a fellow Hmong resident and a CRSS volunteer. Without English and skills for living in an urban, industrialised society, many Hmong struggled at first to find employment and adjust to a new life in Australia.

From the 1970s, Australia also accepted refugees from Europe, the Middle-East, Afghanistan, South and Central America and Africa, most having been displaced from their countries because of internal conflicts and tension, and political, religious and ethnic oppression. Few came direct to Australia, most spending time in other safe countries first.

Sixteen thousand Polish refugees arrived in Australia in the early 1980s. This group had arrived at Melbourne airport in 1983. Mostly young and well-educated, they left Poland, seeking asylum in western Europe initially. They had left Poland ahead of the declaration of martial law in 1981 which suppressed a rising democratic movement led by Solidarity trade unions. Poland was also struggling economically at this time.

Paul was sixteen when he fled Cyprus after Turkey invaded in 1974 and displaced the Greek Cypriot population from the northern half of the island. He was one of fifteen thousand Greek Cypriots who arrived in Australia in the late 1970s and early 1980s. 'When I first came, everything was so flat, and free. Literally, it felt like you were in Paradise, the freedom, the openness.'

Migration Museum interview 1997

Iranians of the Baha'i faith have been accepted into Australia since the early 1980s. They had experienced religious persecution under the fundamentalist Muslim regime which came into power in Iran after the 1979 revolution, ending the reign of the Shah. When the Adelaide *Advertiser* wanted to tell this family's story, the parents kept their backs to the camera for fear that family back home in Iran might have been put at risk.

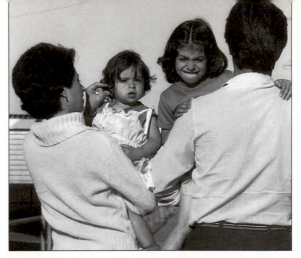

Sri Lankan couple, Rajendran and Rehana Mohanadas arrived in June 1984 under Australia's Special Humanitarian Program following civil tension and violence in Sri Lanka.

During the 1970s and 1980s refugees from a number of south and central American countries found refuge in Australia. Most came from Chile, with others coming from Argentina, Peru, Brazil, Colombia, Uruguay, Mexico and El Salvador. They came to Australia under the Special Humanitarian Program. From both the right and left of politics, they had fled civil war and tension, political, economic and social instability, repressive military regimes, violence, torture and the abuse of human rights. These Chilean children were photographed at Pennington Migrant Hostel (SA) in 1985.

Not everyone who had been displaced from their homelands arrived in Australia either as a refugee or on special humanitarian grounds. Borhan was one of many Kurds who fled from the Turkey, Iran and Iraq border areas. He went first to Romania in 1974, where he was able to study. There he married a Romanian citizen. The family then accepted re-settlement in Denmark before coming to Australia under the General Migration Program in 1988. Borhan identified himself as a refugee.

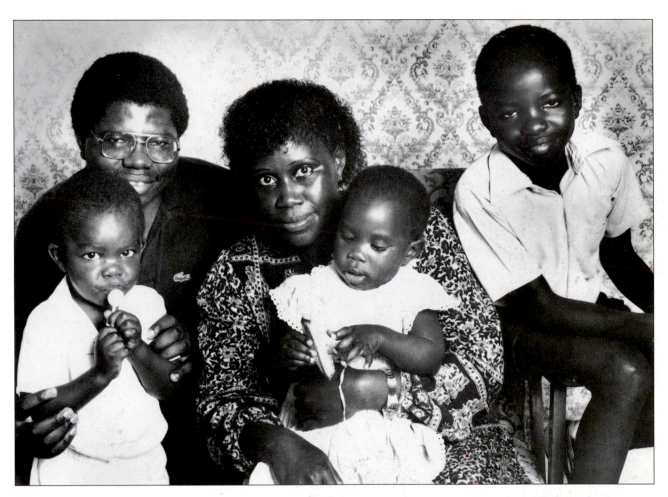

After 1984, Australia accepted small numbers of African refugees in a cautious and restricted program. Most refugees came from Ethiopia. Others were from Uganda, Somalia, Kenya and Ghana. Mostly young, male, literate and from the African middle classes, they had fled civil wars and violence. This Ugandan family arrived in Australia in 1985. They were supported by local Brisbane churches under the Community Refugee Settlement Scheme.

Mohamet Beyan arrived in Darwin in October 1998 from a refugee camp in Kenya where he had fled from Ethiopia in 1991. He had worked as a cook in the camp. Once in Australia, after English classes and recovering from chronic ulcers left untreated in the camp, he began work as a chef at the Discovery Disco in Darwin.

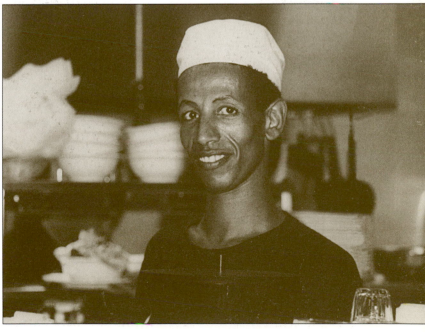

In May 1995 a group of East Timorese arrived in Darwin (NT) on a small fishing boat. They were taken to Curtin Airbase Detention Centre near Derby (WA). Their applications for refugee status were successful. This photograph was taken at Darwin airport after their release. Felipe Silva (left) went to Melbourne where there is a large East Timorese community. Louisa Ferreira (centre) and Jose Gusmao, brother of East Timorese independence leader Xanana Gusmao, stayed in Darwin. They were there in 1999 when East Timorese were airlifted by the Australian government to Darwin after widespread attacks by pro-Indonesian militia following the East Timorese vote for independence from Indonesia.

At the end of the twentieth century, refugees continued to arrive in Australia from new conflicts around the world, with the Australian government maintaining its humanitarian commitment, within set quotas, to assisting those unable to return to their countries.

Croatian, Bosnian and Serbian refugees were accepted as part of Australia's refugee and humanitarian program in the early 1990s as ethnic tension and war engulfed the former Yugoslav republics of Croatia and Bosnia-Herzegovina. The scars of war still showed on the faces of this group attending English classes at the Fairfield Adult Migrant Education Service in Sydney (NSW) in 1996.

In January 1999 seventeen members of the Zenuni family, ethnic Albanians from Kosovo in the Balkans, arrived in Adelaide as refugees. In June 1998, they, and 50 000 others, had fled from their home in Decan in southern Kosovo as Serbian bombs destroyed it. They took little with them as they hid in the surrounding forests and mountains. Terrified, they trekked through Montenegro to a refugee camp in Albania. From there they contacted relatives in Australia who sponsored them to resettle in Australia and raised money for airfares. In an interview with *The Advertiser*, they said: 'We hope to get on with our lives, to continue with our professions and to make a future for ourselves.'

Do Not Forget

Once in Australia, former refugees took the time to remember why they had become refugees. Others exercised their political freedom to protest at the on-going abuse of human rights in their homelands.

In 1975, thirty years after the end of World War II, Australia's Jewish community remembered the Holocaust on Yom Hashoah Day and mourned the loss of their families and communities.

In 1989 members of Sydney's Romanian community demonstrated against the communist regime in Romania, and its record of human rights abuses and political oppression in front of the Romanian Consulate General in Bondi, Sydney.

In a gesture acknowledging the trauma that binds all refugees regardless of origin and date of arrival, former Vietnamese refugees walked in Adelaide in May 1999 to raise money for Albanian Kosovar refugees who had been given temporary asylum in Australia. They had fled from their homeland after violent ethnic cleansing, orchestrated by President Milosevic of the former Yugoslav Republic, swept Kosovo.

Reunited

From the 1970s family reunion, within annual quotas, remained a key element in Australia's immigration program in order to encourage people to settle permanently in Australia.

Family reunion has been especially important for former refugees, separated from family by war and persecution.

In 1977 at Adelaide Airport Than Dui Nguyen and his wife were reunited with three of their five children who had come earlier as refugees to Australia, settling in Adelaide.

At first, the only way for Vietnamese families to be reunited in Australia was through the refugee camps in Thailand and Malaysia. In 1982 the Australian and Vietnamese governments began an 'Orderly Departure Program' direct from Vietnam which allowed families in Australia to sponsor relatives living in Vietnam.

'Family reunion is a part of resettlement, really. I have my family here. They came about three years ago. My brother is a civil engineer, my sisters are teachers. In the future, they will give more and more to Australia. And their children.'

Borhan, former Kurdish refugee, 1996. Migration Museum oral history interview, 1997

When Irish chef, John Boland, immigrated to Australia in 1985, he had arrived on his own, like many young men before him. In another familiar pattern in the immigration story, he then sponsored another family member to join him in Australia. His sister Marie arrived in Australia in 1992. Here they celebrated her Australian citizenship in March 1996.

The four millionth migrant

In 1988 Mai Thanh Thuy (right) arrived from Vietnam to be reunited with her family. She was welcomed as the four millionth migrant assisted to Australia by the Intergovernmental Committee for Migration (ICM, formerly ICEM). She and other settlers from Asian countries arrived at a time of growing tension over Australia's immigration policies. In 1984 historian Geoffrey Blainey created controversy when he voiced concerns over the 'Asianisation' of Australia, although Asian-born settlers were, and continue to be, only a few per cent of the total population. In the mid-late 1990s the same issue was given widespread publicity with the brief rise of the right-wing, anti-Asian immigration One Nation Party led by Pauline Hanson.

Illegal immigrants and refugees

Since its establishment in 1945, the Immigration Department has grappled with the problems associated with illegal immigrants.

Below left: Government estimates in the 1990s suggested that about 50 000 people from many countries including Britain, the United States, Indonesia, the Philippines, Japan and China, were in Australia illegally at any one time. Most had overstayed visas issued for touring, family visits or working holidays. In 1980, in a special amnesty, the Regularisation of Status Program (ROSP), Immigration Minister Ian Macphee, presented a British woman with her letter of approval for permanent residence. She had arrived in 1976 on a working holiday visa.

Bottom: When Indo-Chinese 'boat people' arrived on Australia's shores in the 1970s in the aftermath of the Vietnam conflict, they were granted refugee status and permanent residence. Having endured and fearing on-going communist persecution, they clearly fitted the United Nations guidelines for defining refugees. A group of seventy-nine Cambodian refugees arrived by boat as late as 1990. They were kept in custody for interviews and processing at Camp Currugundi, a scout camp south of Darwin.

In the 1990s more boats landed on Australia's northern shores and outlying territories, bringing people from China, Pakistan, Iran, Iraq, Afghanistan and Sri Lanka. Detention centres filled and new ones opened, such as at Woomera (SA), while immigration authorities began the complex task of establishing their refugee status.

Many 'asylum seekers' were subsequently granted refuge in Australia because of the persecution and oppression they had faced in their homeland. Others were deported, their dreams of a better life in a free, peaceful and democratic society shattered. They had been unable to establish their refugee credentials. Many of them had been the victims of 'people smugglers'.

Throughout the 1990s, human rights organisations criticised the length of time some illegal immigrants had to spend in detention, especially while their appeal against deportation was being heard.

The Federal government also became anxious to prevent the 'floodgates' from opening. It imposed heavy penalties on boat owners, usually Indonesian fishermen, restricted future access to entitlements such as family reunion and began a campaign in the source countries to stem the flow.

Those illegal immigrants who had made it undetected into Australia survived on seasonal work or in unskilled temporary jobs in kitchens and factories where they were vulnerable to exploitation.

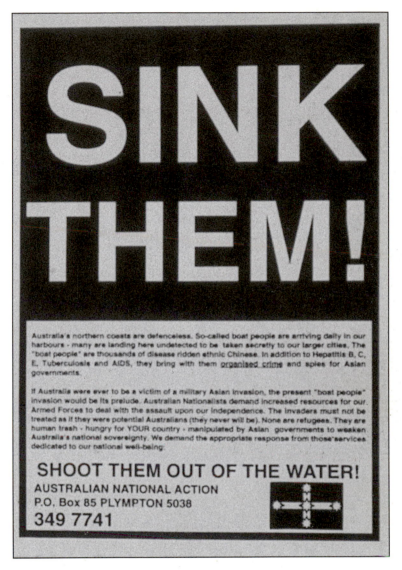

At the end of the 1990s Australians were divided on the issue of 'boat people'. Right-wing fringe groups ran scare campaigns, plastering 'Sink Them!' posters on bus stops and buildings. Others called them 'queue jumpers' who jeopardised Australia's on-going refugee and humanitarian programs. Many extended a compassionate and welcoming hand. Government authorities and the Australian people recognised also that illegal entry and the status of these arrivals would continue to be a major issue into the 21st century.

To be seen and heard

By the mid 1970s overseas-born residents had become an obvious presence in Australian society. They began to demand that their needs be acknowledged and catered for.

Although the Department of Immigration had always taken a role in assisting immigrants to settle in, this focus was greatly expanded. The Department's name was changed to include reference to ethnic and later multicultural affairs.

In the interests of social justice and equity for all Australians, both Federal and state governments devised policies which addressed the specific needs of immigrants, in the work force and in the community, regardless of origin or cultural background. Such policies had bipartisan political support and were designed to woo the migrant vote.

Al Grassby, (centre front), Minister for Immigration in the Whitlam government, was one of the first to describe Australia as a multicultural society. He advocated political and social change to make Australian society vibrant, tolerant and inclusive. He was photographed in 1973 with a Queensland Task Force established to identify and recommend solutions to problems faced by immigrants. The Task Force included prominent Anglo-Celtic academics, social workers, Good Neighbour Council volunteers and Department for Immigration branch directors. Two post-war migrants were also to be appointed.

Immigrant voices were not the only voices demanding social justice and equality of opportunity. Indigenous Australians campaigned for the return of their traditional lands, for an end to institutional racism, for better health services and housing, and access to education. In 1972 Aboriginal activists erected a tent embassy on the lawns in front of Parliament House in Canberra (ACT) to raise awareness of Aboriginal demands and to force the government to improve their political, social and economic position.

At this time, women and people with disabilities also demanded recognition, social justice and equality. In response, governments passed significant reform legislation, including the 1975 *Racial Discrimination Act* and established consultative bodies.

The Changing Face of Australia

In languages other than English

Governments acknowledged that settlers continued to use their own languages in Australia and that the use of community languages actually assisted new arrivals to adjust to a new life in Australia.

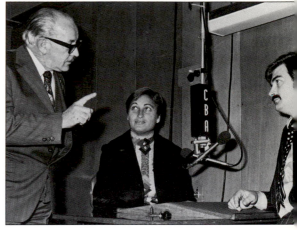

Above: Radio and television services were established to provide programs, films, local and overseas news services, sports coverage and information in many languages. From 1975 radio stations, at first 2EA in Sydney, 3EA in Melbourne and then across Australia, began to broadcast programs in community languages. These were largely an initiative of the communities themselves and self-funded. In 1978 the Australian government established Special Broadcasting Service (SBS), a radio and television service to provide programs, films, local and overseas news services, sports coverage and information in many languages.

In 1973 a 24-hour Telephone Interpreter Service was established across Australia for non-English speaking settlers and private and public agencies. Government departments, in particular, began to provide essential information in a number of key languages. The Department of Immigration employed Bilingual Information Officers to provide new arrivals with information about government services and community networks.

Access and equity

From the late 1970s an extensive network of community services, both government-funded and community-funded, combined with conferences, seminars, discussion papers, committees, project officers, welfare workers and grant-in-aid workers, among other methods, sought to address the specific needs of particular sections of the migrant population. These included refugees, victims of torture and trauma, older persons, women, newly arrived settlers, non-English speaking immigrants and youth. This network became an important source of paid employment and voluntary work for many Australians.

The allocation of government resources and the presence of politicians and government ministers at openings and a myriad of community functions attested to the growing importance that political parties placed on wooing the migrant vote.

'A Fair Go for Ethnic Youth' conference in 1982 was organised by the Youth Affairs council of New South Wales as part of a project to develop models of working with migrant youth and to train youth workers to apply these models.

The Canterbury/ Bankstown Migrant Resource Centre in Campsie (NSW), opened in 1987 by Mick Young, Minister for Immigration and Ethnic Affairs in the Hawke Labor government, was one of many established across Australia from the late 1970s. These centres were funded by government to attend to the welfare needs of diverse immigrant groups in response to the recommendations of the 1978 Galbally Report, *The Review of Post-Arrival Programs and Services for Migrants*.

With the development of Migrant Resource Centres and other community-based organisations catering for the needs of increasingly diverse, non-English speaking groups, The Good Neighbour Movement, established in 1949 primarily to 'assimilate' new British arrivals and Displaced Persons into the community, became largely redundant. Government support was withdrawn in 1978, and as a consequence most Good Neighbour Council offices closed.

Below: At Botany (NSW) Migrant Resource Centre in 1986 a group of Italian Australians enjoyed a game of bingo together. Ten years later in 1996 this group was still meeting every Thursday morning, testimony to the continuity of services in Migrant Resource Centres.

Self-help and self-management became the catch cry in the 1980s.

In 1983 a group of Filipino women gathered for a self-help session, addressing marital, family, employment and communication problems that they and other Filipino women encountered in Australia. At this time about half of the Filipino women settling in Australia were sponsored by Australian men to whom they were engaged or newly married.

In 1988 these children attended the Acacia Indo-Chinese Child Care Centre in Richmond (Vic), a Melbourne suburb with a high concentration of Vietnamese settlers. Many community organisations established their own child care centres, providing women in particular with the chance to work and supplement the family income. By the late 1990s many of these centres faced problems associated with rising costs and fluctuating government support.

Multiculturalism: the national agenda

In July 1989 in Canberra Prime Minister Bob Hawke, flanked by staff of the Office of Multicultural Affairs, launched the National Agenda for a Multicultural Society. Until then, although the term 'multicultural' had been used with increasing frequency to describe Australian society, it was loosely defined and had limited and ad hoc influence on government and community practice. The 1989 Agenda acknowledged the cultural diversity of Australian society and set principles to guide future governments, employer groups and community organisations in ensuring that their policies and structures reflected that diversity.

Multiculturalism became a household word. For the majority of Australians, it was a welcome blueprint for social harmony that showcased Australia as a tolerant, 'clever' society, but some saw it as a recipe for social division and a dilution of the Australian identity. Many Anglo-Celtic Australians misunderstood its intent, believing that Multiculturalism did not encompass them and their heritage.

Many Indigenous Australians felt that with Multiculturalism they would be regarded as 'just another ethnic group' and lose their right to be specially acknowledged as Australia's First Peoples.

In 1989 the Hawke Labor government established the Bureau of Immigration Research (BIR) to gather and distribute information on Australia's immigrants. Under the following Labor government of Paul Keating, the Bureau was renamed the Bureau of Immigration, Multicultural and Population Research and became a key player in the implementation of the policy of multiculturalism. The Liberal government of Prime Minister John Howard, elected to power in 1996, closed BIMPR, reflecting a change in government attitudes and priorities.

Governments in the 1990s implemented the policy of Multiculturalism with differing levels of commitment. On the whole, Multiculturalism was proudly accepted by Australians as an accurate reflection of the culturally diverse society they lived and worked in.

Immigrants unite!

In the 1970s community clubs and associations became more political in focus. They began to lobby government for funds to run self-help programs such as aged care facilities, language schools for their children and to employ specialist staff for a wide variety of health and welfare programs. They relied, to a large extent, on the volunteer efforts of members.

For more effective liaison with other organisations and government, most joined national 'umbrella' organisations such as Ethnic Communities Councils which, in turn, were affiliated with the Federation of Ethnic Communities Councils of Australia (FECCA).

FECCA was established in 1979 as a non-political, non-profit voluntary organisation whose mission was 'to enrich and enhance the wellbeing of the Australian community, through the fullest participation and involvement of people of diverse cultural and ethnic backgrounds, especially those who have experienced the migration process'.

In 1997, placards carried in the Turkish Day Parade in Sydney for the Australia-Turkish Festival revealed just a few of the Turkish organisations established to support and assist Turkish residents in New South Wales.

Below right: In 1998 the Prime Minister John Howard and Minister for Immigration and Multicultural Affairs Minister, Philip Ruddock, continued a government tradition of meeting with FECCA.

This group represented twenty years of advocacy on behalf of Australia's ethnic groups. Whereas members were once mostly from European countries, the 1999 membership reflected the growing influence of Asian settlers, although newer settler groups were not yet represented. In 1999, FECCA was also largely male-dominated, as were many of Australia's political organisations, raising the question of whether the needs of all of Australia's overseas-born settlers were being sufficiently represented to government.

Working lives

In the 1950s and 60s there was plenty of work for new settlers. From the 1970s finding work became a challenge in an economy dominated by recession, restructuring, insecurity and job losses. Skilled and professional workers recruited to fill skills gaps in the Australian work force generally found work quickly after arrival. It was harder for refugees or those who arrived on special humanitarian programs, as they were most likely to arrive without English, from rural backgrounds and from years in refugee camps where their education was disrupted. Commonwealth and State governments became anxious to reduce the welfare budget and offset public criticism of immigrants and refugees being a burden on the taxpayer. They began to fund intensive English language programs and computer skills programs to hasten the entry of new arrivals into the work force.

A 1996 Literacy for Work class applauded its graduates at Fairfield (NSW) Adult Migrant Education Service. For many years, Fairfield in Sydney has had a high concentration of new settlers from many backgrounds. Participants in classes at the Fairfield AMES in 1996 included settlers from Vietnam, China, the Slovak Republic, Bosnia, Serbia, the Philippines, Cambodia and Iraq (including Assyrians).

After opening in 1981 Fairfield AMES conducted English language classes and skills programs such as computing and operated a day care centre for children whose parents attended classes. Many participants arrived as refugees or on the Family Reunion program.

The graduation ceremony was a moment full of hope. But the picture was incomplete. The story for the new graduates and their efforts to secure work continued beyond the classroom and beyond the cameras that recorded their graduation.

In the late 1980s, the Middle East Co-operative in Glenroy, a Melbourne suburb, was an initiative of the Lebanese community, set up with government help, to combat unemployment in the Lebanese community, many of whom had arrived in Australia under the special humanitarian program.

Factory work remained a traditional source of unskilled employment for newly arrived immigrants, especially those with non-English speaking backgrounds. This worker at the Ford car assembly plant at Broadmeadows in Melbourne (VIC) found work within two weeks of arriving in Australia from Lebanon in 1988.

Below: Like many others, these two Laotian women picking cucumbers at Virginia (SA), found seasonal work on market gardens. The property owners had arrived from Vietnam in the late 1970s as refugees and worked as pickers for local Greek and Italian growers who had settled there in the 1950s. As the Italian and Greek growers retired, so Vietnamese settlers purchased the properties. Across Australia the history of market gardens and fruit blocks has reflected the changing waves of immigrants and refugees who have settled in Australia.

THE CHANGING FACE OF AUSTRALIA

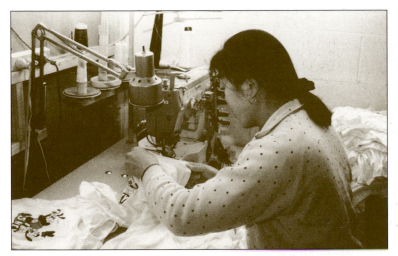

Other unskilled arrivals had no choice but to take on outwork. They knitted, sewed or assembled lamps and other goods over long hours for little pay in their own homes. They worked in isolation and many felt powerless to prevent exploitation by unscrupulous bosses. The nature of the work meant that they often suffered repetitive strain injuries. Over the 1980s and 1990s the Textile Clothing and Footwear Union worked to improve award protection for outworkers, increase employers' obligations and to inform outworkers of their rights.

Immigrants have always been strongly represented in food processing industries. Most of the women packing glacé fruit in this factory in 1984 were immigrants from southern European countries. They had arrived in Australia some years before.

In the 20th century, Australian trade unions have been generally wary about immigration and slow to respond, especially in the 1950s and 60s, to the needs of their overseas-born members, despite their significant presence in many industries. In times of economic depression or high unemployment, unions actively campaigned against immigration as contributing to Australian job losses. In line with the National Agenda for a Multicultural Australia, unions since the late 1980s began to acknowledge overseas-born workers and address their specific needs.

Many of the immigrants who arrived in the 1950s and 60s remained in factory work or cleaning jobs for their working lives. They worked hard, often taking on more than one job. They did it to give their children a better education. The Australian-born generation were the ones to go on to university and move into the white-collar sector and into the professions. Graduation photographs became proof that Australia indeed offered a better life, if not for themselves, then for their children.

A matter of business

As with previous generations of immigrants, working hard in a small business was an opportunity to achieve economic security in Australia.

In the early 1970s Turkish settler, Kemal Yuceturk (in white shirt), found a niche in the market and opened a driving school for other Turkish settlers in Parramatta (NSW). For many Turkish settlers driving was a new experience but essential for daily and working life in suburban Australia. The name of his business was designed to attract Turkish-born learner drivers, but his car was strictly Australian-made.

Growing fruit and vegetables or selling them has, in particular, dominated the small business sector for new arrivals.

Above: Dahn Son, originally from Vietnam, became a self-employed market gardener at Geraldton (WA) where he was photographed in 1994 for a special exhibition organised by the Battye Library in Perth on the cultural diversity of Western Australian workers.

In Darwin in 1992 three Vietnamese business partners began to grow oyster mushrooms, mostly for the local market, in a shed on the outskirts of Darwin. The business was successful but the profits weren't enough to support all three partners in the long term. Two years later, after they had found full-time jobs, they closed the mushroom business that had given them their start in Australia.

Thi My Pham and her husband Tan Khiet Huynh established a fruit and vegetable shop in suburban Adelaide. They had arrived as 'boat people', living and working first of all in Sydney, eventually settling in Adelaide. They then sponsored other members of their extended family to Australia. It was especially important for them, the success of their business and the upbringing of their children to have grandparents join them in Australia.

Sometimes businesses have directly reflected a settler's cultural origins.

In the 1980s Japanese couple Shinichi and Tomoko Shibuya opened a sushi bar in Ivanhoe, a Melbourne suburb. With only small numbers of Japanese settlers in Australia, their customers came from other backgrounds.

The Ayoubi family, originally from Lebanon, opened their nut store in the Melbourne suburb of Brunswick to cater for the many Lebanese Australians living in the local area.

In order to find work in Australia some settlers had to discard previous experience or qualifications. This was a frustrating and humiliating experience. Often their qualifications were not recognised in Australia and retraining was out of the question due to family responsibilities. Dr Vihn Quoc An, a doctor in Vietnam, was able to go back to study and requalify as a doctor in Australia. In the 1980s he opened a medical practice in Richmond, a Melbourne suburb with a large Vietnamese population.

Many small businesses started by new settlers expanded to become significant employers of new arrivals and others.

The Chien Wah factory in Melbourne, producing spring rolls, dim sims and other Chinese food, became an example of business success.

Some businesses expanded onto the international market. By the 1990s, the San Remo pasta factory, established by Luigi Crotti in Adelaide in the 1940s, was beginning to establish markets in Italy and countries in South-East Asia.

Multicultural Australia

In the 1970s clubs and associations began to flourish. Especially in the larger groups, the immigrant generation of the 1950s and 60s and their Australian-born children created a vibrant close-knit social life within their communities. With increasing public and government recognition of the place of immigrants in Australian society, there was a new pride and confidence in owning one's ethnicity.

Above: The Italian Club in Sydney by the early 1970s had grown into an extensive complex, with bocce courts and playgrounds. Many of the larger and well-established settler groups were building multi-purpose clubrooms with rooms for theatre and music performances, with libraries, dining rooms, large catering kitchens and space for wedding receptions.

In a wide variety of community clubs and associations, there were sporting groups, youth groups, and music, dance and theatrical performances. They thrived on volunteer committees and fundraising efforts. They were part and parcel of Australia's community life.

Below: There in the clubrooms the younger Australian-born generation learnt the dances and the songs of their parents' homeland. Parents and grandparents felt a sense of pride and achievement in passing on these cultural traditions.

Romanian Mihai Maghiaru watched his son, Gabriel, dance at Sydney's Romanian club in 1976. It was 10 May, Romanian National Day and the 25th anniversary of the establishment of the Australian Romanian Association. It was a proud day for Mihai.

But what were the traditions to be passed down to the next generation? The young Greek girls dancing at the laying of the foundation stone for Sydney's Castellorizian social club in 1972 gave a very modern interpretation to the dances of their forebears.

Throughout the 20th century immigrants formed and joined clubs to spend time with people who shared the same cultural traditions and to keep those traditions alive for their children and grandchildren.

But as with all things, clubs have had to confront the changes that occur in society over time. At the end of the 20th century, clubs formed by the immigrants of the 1950s and 60s struggled to keep up numbers as original members aged and the Australian-born generations became busy with other priorities. Some of the clubs began to operate their facilities and clubrooms as a commercial business, attracting the broader local community, in order to survive. Other clubs closed, their properties sold.

The extensive Australia-wide network of ethnic organisations remained a strong feature of community life in Australia at the end of the 20th century, as newer arrivals founded their own clubs and joined umbrella organisations established by previous generations of immigrants. Some of the newest clubs were established over the last decade by arrivals from the former USSR, the Middle-East, Pacific Islands and African countries.

Diversity and difference

A consequence of a century of immigration has been the emergence of a culturally diverse society. Food, religious observance, festivals and celebrations, sport and the arts have reflected that diversity.

Chops and Changes: Food, Immigrants and Culture

Since the beginning of the post-war mass migration program, immigrants have had a profound effect on the food Australians eat. Before then, Australians largely followed British culinary traditions, although they made changes in response to Australian conditions.

European immigrants in the 1950s and 60s prepared and cooked the food that had been a part of their way of life back home. Some of the vegetables and herbs they grew in their backyards. Soon continental delicatessens, bakeries and butcher shops opened up to sell the foodstuffs that they couldn't grow themselves. Other stores sold the special utensils they needed. Restaurants and cafes opened up, initially to give settler groups the tastes and cosmopolitan style of the homelands they'd left. As a consequence, the Australians who were tempted to try new foods broadened their eating habits.

This shift in Australian eating habits meant success for continental food stores. And success too for the shops and restaurants opened up by Asian settlers after their arrival from the late 1970s.

Below: When Lina D'Aprano fetched her bottled sauce from the cellar of her Melbourne home in 1988 to make a pasta sauce, she was continuing a familiar practice based on the regional food traditions of her Italian homeland. Ten years later, Stefano de Pieri, a chef from Mildura (VIC), took the food traditions of local Italian settlers and created a popular television program, *A Gondola on the Murray*. Its popularity was largely due to the fact that Australians by the 1990s had come to embrace the food traditions of many lands.

Food traditions are both a private and public 'affare'.

By the late 1990s in Australian backyards, next to the barbecue, there were wood-fired ovens for pizza and bread or tandoor ovens for baking chapatis and naan bread (shown above).

At their 'Sala Thai' stall at the Rapid Creek Sunday markets in Darwin in July 1999, Chi and Ratchanee Warawitya prepared Thai food for sale. For Chi (stirring food) and Ratchanee, cooking and selling food in Darwin markets was part of their migration story. They had come from Thailand in 1988 to ensure a better education for their children. 'I died so my kids could be reborn', said Chi.

Spires, cupolas and minarets

Religious practice in Australia changed with waves of immigrants. In 1900 Australians were overwhelmingly Christians, either Protestants or Catholics. The immigrants of the 1950s and 60s added to the ranks of these churches.

The arrival of settlers from Asian and Middle-Eastern countries over the last thirty years of the 20th century increased the number of Australians who followed the Hindu, Muslim and Buddhist faiths. Freedom of religious association was cherished by many new arrivals, whether Christian Assyrians, or Russian Orthodox or Iranian Baha'i.

Above: Other settlers in the 1950s and 60s, including Greek, Russian, Belarusian, Bulgarian, Ukrainian, Egyptian, Serbian, Romanian and Macedonian arrivals, belonged to Orthodox Christian communities. By the early 1970s many of these groups, with volunteer fundraising efforts and labour, had built substantial churches. In Melbourne in 1973, Bishop Kyril, Metropolitan of the Macedonian Orthodox Diocese of Canada, America and Australia, blessed a gathering of over 3000 Macedonian Australians at the laying of the foundation stone for the first Macedonian Orthodox monastery in Australia.

In 1980, an Indian family celebrated the birth of a baby with a Hindu naming ceremony.

Indo-Chinese settlers opened up their
Buddhist temples across Australia. This
temple, shown here in 1985, was in Sydney
where many Vietnamese and Cambodian
refugees settled.

The mosque in Auburn, a Sydney suburb, was built in the 1980s by the local Turkish Muslim settlers. Along with other mosques, it added to the myriad shapes of Australia's architectural heritage. But it was by no means the first mosque in Australia. The first ones were built in the 1880s by 'Afghan' camel drivers in South Australia where they had settled since the 1860s.

The arrival of Muslim settlers from Middle-Eastern, Asian and European countries during the last thirty years of the 20th century renewed and strengthened the observance of the Muslim faith in Australia. This renewal began with the arrival of Turkish settlers from the late 1960s. Muslim Australians have sometimes been the target of racist sentiment from sections of the Australian community resistant to the increasing diversity of new arrivals.

A service marking the canonisation of one hundred and seventeen Vietnamese Catholic martyrs at St Patrick's Cathedral in Melbourne in 1988 epitomised how immigrants also diversified the dominant Anglo-Celtic Protestant and Catholic religions. Settlers from Asian countries such as Korea, China, India and Vietnam, for a long time a focus of European Christian missionary activity, joined Protestant and Catholic congregations. Lebanese Australians brought the Melkite and Maronite Catholic traditions to Australia. Egyptian Christians, Copts, also settled in Australia since the late 1960s.

The family has also been key to the maintenance of religious observance. Here in 1988 in Sydney a Jewish family gathered around the table for the Sabbath meal.

For some cultural groups religious observance has been a unifying force. The familiar rituals and language have offered stability, comfort and links with the home country. For other communities religion has not been a focus for activity. Religious observance has been essentially an individual commitment. Many Australians, of many backgrounds, have not taken part in any religious activities at all. Others have been devoted to their faith.

Changing traditions

Traditions have changed in a new landscape, over the
generations and for each person over their lifespan.

From the turn of the century, fishermen from Molfetta on the Adriatic Sea had settled in Port Pirie, bringing with them a devotion to Our Lady of Martyrs. For generations, Italians in Molfetta held a religious festival, with Masses and a procession, to seek her protection of the fishing fleet, the economic lifeblood of the town. The religious formalities ended with a fair.

As the small Italian fishing community grew in Port Pirie in the 1930s, they brought out a statue of Our Lady and each year held the Masses in the local Catholic church. At first there was no procession or fair. That was beyond their resources. In the late 1940s, when more Molfettesi arrived, they held a procession on the local oval. In 1956, feeling more confident of their place in the town, they took Our Lady's statue out onto the streets of Port Pirie and onto the waters of the harbour.

The annual Blessing of the Fleet continued on through the years, taking on a distinctive Australian flavour. Rather than a fair, the community held a concert or a ball. Often it was a debutante ball, an English tradition popular in Australian country towns.

But by 1988, when these photographs were taken, there were very few Molfettese fishermen left in Port Pirie. There was no fishing fleet to bless. Many of the younger generations had moved on to other work, often in other places. In 1988, the Blessing of the Fleet was part of the town's official Bicentennial celebrations. The local mayor and other dignitaries attended. The significance of the Blessing of the Fleet had changed. In Fremantle, another fishing port where Italians from Molfetta had settled, the ceremony had even become a tourist attraction.

This sporting life

Sport in Australia has reflected the social and cultural changes that have occurred as part of the migration and settlement process.

In the 1950s and 60s sporting loyalties were largely divided. Just taking the football codes as an example, Anglo-Celtic Australians played and watched rugby and Australian Rules football. European settlers followed soccer, with teams often based on national origins.

By the 1990s competitive sports, played at both the elite and local club level, came to involve players from many different backgrounds. Devoted fans became just as diverse, with television and marketing probably determining spectator interest and team loyalty more than ethnicity.

Immigrants introduced a diversity of sports and games. A friendly game of petanque among Adelaide's French settlers in 1988 was fiercely contested, with close attention paid to correctly measuring the distance between the bowls and the target to determine the winner.

In Italy, it was the men who played bocce, not women. In Australia, these women from an Italian club in Sydney in 1972 broke with tradition and formed their own competition. Before then, a photograph of women playing bocce would have been unheard of.

From the 1980s dragon boat racing became a competitive sport in Australia. This was a far cry from the origins of the races in a southern Chinese Buddhist Festival held to commemorate the death of Qu Yen, a righteous man who drowned himself in 314BC in the Mek Lo River in protest at the corruption of the Imperial Court. The local villagers who had a deep respect for Qu Yen held dragon boat races to honour him and keep evil spirits away so that he remained at peace in the river. Winning and training weren't important. Of greater importance was the lesson Qu Yen gave on how people should live their lives.

Out in the streets

By the 1990s, at any time of the year, anywhere across Australia, on streets and in parks, multicultural carnivals and festivals had become a familiar fixture of the Australian weekend. It might have been a Polish Harvest Festival or a Greek Glenti or a multicultural mixture.

By the late 1970s, as governments began to cater for the specific needs of settler groups, there was a corresponding wider public acceptance of difference in cultural lifestyles. Immigrants felt more confident. It was okay to 'go public' with your language, food traditions, music, dance, arts and crafts. Federal and state governments, local councils and businesses sponsored community groups to make the festivals an economic success. Many festivals became tourist attractions.

Multicultural carnivals changed cultural traditions. There was often a vast difference between what was presented at public multicultural festivals and what was still celebrated at home and at the club.

There was a fear, too, that such festivals stereotyped immigrants and overshadowed the real and diverse contributions made by immigrants to Australian life.

In 1979 the Italians of Carlton (Vic) held a festa in Lygon Street. It was a public celebration of the food, wine and music that had been nurtured within Italian families and clubs since Italian settlers had first arrived in the district. Assimilation had gone, replaced with a celebration of difference. Such festivals became popular because the arrivals of the 1950s and 60s had the time, resources and confidence to organise them.

The Lygon Street festa changed over the years. Other cultural groups became involved. It was no longer a purely Italian festival. Although some of the organisers expressed regret at these changes, others understood that change was inevitable as the make-up of the local population changed.

Above: In February 1988 this group of Finnish
Australians participated in the Sydney
Carnival, in the procession and folk-dancing.

In Brisbane in 1996 dancers from many
cultures performed at a multicultural festival.

Opposite: At a Turkish Day Parade in Sydney in 1997 Fatma Yucel, who had come from Cyprus in 1985, handed out Turkish Delights. As well as participating in local Turkish associations and events, Fatma also contributed to Australian society, professionally as a mechanical engineer and in employment as a high school teacher.

In 1996 Spanish Australians attracted many participants and tourists to their annual pilgrimage at Clare (SA) in honour of La Virgen del Rocio. The Clare Valley reminded Spaniards of the landscape of their homeland, but the woman in the Drizabone coat (centre) gave the event a truly Australian flavour.

The Changing Face of Australia

Opposite: Throughout the 20th century, immigrants made significant contributions to Australia's civic and community life, very often on a voluntary basis. Peg Parkin, who arrived from Britain in the 1960s, became mayor of the City of Belmont in Perth in the 1980s. She was typical of the many overseas-born settlers who over the years became mayors or councillors in their local area.

In 1994 members of Sydney's Romanian community dedicated their annual picnic to raising funds for the New South Wales Bush Fire Appeal. This was only one example of the way that overseas-born Australians frequently, with generosity and concern, expressed their sense of unity with fellow Australians regardless of cultural background, especially in time of need.

The end of the century: the arrivals board

At the beginning of the 20th century the vast majority of immigrants to Australia had come from Britain and Ireland. At the end of the century, immigrants from Britain and Ireland were still at the top of the arrivals list, but were, overall, a much smaller proportion of total arrivals who were coming from numerous source countries.

Three arrivals in the 1990s, from Africa, from Tatarstan and from England, represented some of the changes and trends in Australian immigration patterns at the end of the century.

In the 1970s most immigrants came from Britain and Ireland, Yugoslavia, New Zealand, Lebanon, the United States of America and Greece, with forty per cent coming from Britain and Ireland. In the 1980s, most came from Britain and Ireland, New Zealand, Viet Nam, the Philippines, South Africa and Poland, with 20 per cent from Britain and Ireland. In the 1990s, the biggest arrival groups were from Britain and Ireland, New Zealand, China, Hong Kong, Viet Nam and the Philippines, with 12 per cent from Britain and Ireland.

Arrivals from Africa

In the 1970s and 80s most African arrivals, especially from South Africa and Kenya, were European or Asian. In the 1990s small numbers of indigenous Africans, especially from Ethiopia, Somalia, Sudan, Nigeria and Ghana, began to arrive under immigration and refugee programs. They faced initial problems of unemployment and homesickness. Many encountered racism. Emerging African community organisations became an important source of support.

On their first day in Australia, a Sudanese family was welcomed and shown around Sydney by a representative of the African Communities Council in New South Wales. Their arrival was in stark contrast with the beginning of the century when the Australian government implemented strategies to keep Australia white.

Arrivals from Europe

The arrival of immigrants from Asian, Middle-Eastern, African and Pacific countries became the trend in the last three decades of the 20th century. Europe provided fewer of Australia's new settlers. Forty and fifty years earlier, large numbers came from countries such as Italy, Greece, Germany and the Netherlands. In the 1990s, settlers from Europe arrived in smaller numbers but from an increasing diversity of countries, including Poland, Romania, the Czech and Slovak Republics and the former Union of Soviet Socialist Republics.

Irek Garipov (centre back) came to Australia from Kazan, the capital of Tatarstan in 1992, to join his wife Musharraf (back left) whom he had married shortly before. Musharraf, an Australian citizen, had arrived in Australia in 1981 with her mother (front right) and family on a United Nations program to resettle China's White Russian residents. They had met in 1989 in Kazan when Musharraf returned there to visit relatives. Irek was then a leader of the Young Tatar Movement fighting for political and cultural freedom for all Tatars. Irek and Musharraf posed in 1995 with their three children, Musharaff's mother and Irek's mother (front left) who had come to Australia to visit them. For Irek, Australia had given him and his family the freedom to wear their national dress and to teach their children their language and traditions.

An arrival from Britain: Mark's story

In 1999 Mark Pharaoh sat on the front gate of his Adelaide home. He had arrived from Britain in the 1990s, his British place of birth putting him into the mainstream of Australia's immigration history. Mark's story revealed links with many other immigrants who have settled in Australia in the 20th century.

Migrants are adventurers and risk takers.

Mark was born in 1966 into a Royal Air Force family and moved a lot, from West Berlin to Scotland, London, East Anglia, the Midlands and Cyprus.

As a young man, he travelled and worked overseas. He was impressed by the adventurous Australians he met on his travels, including 'Frosty', a South Australian he met in Egypt in 1988. In 1991 Mark came to Australia on a working visa to catch up with Australians he had met. Landing first in Perth, he hitchhiked his way to Darwin and Alice Springs where he caught the 'Ghan' to Adelaide to catch up with friends there.

Seasonal work has given many arrivals their first taste of Australia.

In Adelaide he met his future wife Jill through mutual friends. Together they travelled around Australia, taking on seasonal work as fruit pickers. In Batlow (NSW) Mark was photographed loading apples into crates, a job done by so many other young single men who had arrived before him seeking work in Australia. The advice Mark received was that 'if you don't do this in Australia, then you're missing out on an essential Australian experience'.

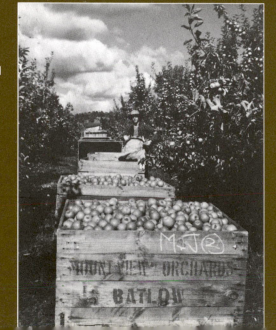

Migration is about opportunities and new beginnings.

At the end of his working visa, Mark returned to England, taking Jill, a horticulturalist, with him. They studied and worked in Nottingham in the Midlands. There was plenty of work for them in England, although Jill found it hard working outdoors in the English winter. They made the decision to live in Australia, trading off better career prospects in England against the healthy lifestyle and warmer climate of Australia.

Early in 1993 Mark applied to come to Australia as a permanent resident. In December 1993, with friends and relatives from Australia, England and the United States, they married in an outdoor garden ceremony.

'I miss the history and landscape of England terribly. But what compensates is the climate and different landscape of Australia, and its equally rich and fascinating history so full of contradictions.' Mark Pharaoh, 1999.

Migrants make choices for their children's future.

Mark and Jill decided to live in Adelaide because 'it's a nice place to bring up a family'. Reuben was born in September 1996. 'It's only recently dawned on me that I'd like Reuben to have an Aussie accent. That would make him a foreigner in England. His home is Australia'.

Establishing a home is a priority for immigrants and is a sign of commitment to their adopted country.

Mark and Jill purchased a renovator's delight of a home in Adelaide. The *For Sale* sign said it had 'loads of potential'. The hard work involved in demolishing and rebuilding the house is symbolic for Mark of the re-building and re-creation of himself that was part of his migration journey. According to Mark, this was a task 'not to be undertaken lightly'.

2000
REASONS TO REMEMBER

A century of immigration changed Australia from an overwhelmingly Anglo-Celtic society to a culturally diverse one, although Anglo-Celtic Australians still formed a majority of the population. With a quarter of the population born overseas and another quarter with one or more parents born overseas, the immigration experience remained close to home for many Australians.

At the 1996 Census, in a nation of over 18.3 million people, 3.9 million people had been born overseas in one of over 200 countries. A further 3.8 million had one or both parents born overseas. There were 2.6 million people who spoke a language other than English at home. The 1996 Census classified 92 religious denominations as well as 282 major languages, including 170 Aboriginal and Torres Strait Islander languages.

When Alice Springs women celebrated International Women's Day with a parade of costumes, they acknowledged their different origins but highlighted their common bond as women in Australia.

Being an Australian

A century of immigration created a vibrant and complex society, with many ways of being an Australian and recognising the ties that bind.

Most Australians acknowledge their ethnicity. It has become part and parcel of being an Australian. It has become one way that Australians connect with the past, share a sense of belonging with others and shape the pattern of their lives. Australians move between groups and identities, between global, community and family influences. Children at the 20th century's end have epitomised this process.

Above: In 1995 in Alice Springs, women from different cultures shared some of their craft skills at a Multicultural Arts Workshop.

This little Chinese girl, participating in a Chinese display in Little Bourke Street for Melbourne's Moomba Festival in the late 1970s, was celebrating the culture and heritage of her forebears who had come to Australia over a century earlier and had lived and worked in the same area.

In 1994 for Kathryn Horacek of Tasmania dressing in her Czech national costume was one way of connecting with the cultural traditions her grandparents had brought to Australia as Displaced Persons at the end of World War II.

Two little girls waited their turn at a multicultural festival in Brisbane in 1996 to perform the dances of their parents' Pacific homeland.

'Have fun with your roots' was the message Egyptian-born Morris Mansour (right) passed on to his children.

In the late 1990s, many Australian children attended ethnic schools, especially on weekends, to learn the language, stories, history, dances and songs of the homeland of their parents or grandparents. They belonged to close-knit community organisations. Their ethnicity was an important part of their daily lives. These children, posing with their parents, teachers and community leaders, attended the Tatar-Bashkurt Ethnic School in Adelaide.

At the same time, for other Australian children, their ethnicity was largely a symbolic gesture, confined to special occasions. It was a part of their family history, without having a significant impact on the pattern of their daily lives.

This New South Wales family wore their Cornish tartan to the 1999 Kernewek Lowender, Cornish festival, in South Australia's 'Little Cornwall'. They were revisiting the history and heritage of their Cornish forebears who had lived and worked in the mining townships of Wallaroo, Kadina and Moonta in the 19th century.

Children at the end of the 20th century shared interests, diets and skills formed by the global youth culture which took them beyond their local community and family and connected them with the wider world. Computer games, the Internet and fast food outlets took them into other cultural practices that had little to do with their ethnicity or migrant heritage.

At the end of the 20th century, it has become
commonplace for Australians to have spouses
or partners with a cultural background
different from their own. Many Australian
families shared more than one ethnicity as
part of their heritage, with cultural practices
negotiated, combined, or transformed into
something distinctively belonging to
that family.

Keeping the landscape and the history

Wherever immigrants settled they made an impact on their environment.

In many instances the evidence of that history disappeared, especially in earlier decades when the contribution of immigrants was largely unacknowledged. Since the late 1980s, local councils, businesses and building owners, in conjunction with government agencies whose brief it is to preserve the evidence of Australia's past, took steps to identify and preserve the buildings and streetscapes that were part of Australia's migrant heritage.

From the 1970s Vietnamese settlers changed the streetscape of Victoria Road in Richmond, a Melbourne suburb. In nearby Carlton, Lygon Street bore the stamp of earlier Italian settlers. In the bayside suburb of St Kilda, Acland Street had its pastry shops and cafes opened by Jewish settlers. Little Bourke Street in the heart of Melbourne continued to be associated with Chinese Australians whose forebears came to Victoria in the middle of the 19th century. Streetscapes such as these could be found in cities, suburbs and towns around Australia.

Some communities opened up their own museums and historical archives in order to document, preserve and create awareness of the history of their immigrant forebears. They joined a network of local and regional museums around Australia.

Descendants of early Chinese settlers in the Northern Territory, including (from left) Jeremy Chin, Daryl Chin and Des Yuen established the Chung Wah Museum in Darwin in 1996. They wanted the Museum to serve as a reminder to future generations of the important part Chinese settlers played in the development of the Northern Territory. As the Chung Wah Society acknowledged in their brochure: 'They faced extreme hardships and discrimination but their determination and perseverance to overcome these difficulties have earned them a place in history'.

In April 1999, in a ceremony honouring their ancestors, Vietnamese South Australians placed a plaque on the memorial wall at Adelaide's Migration Museum. The plaque recorded the reasons why they had fled their homeland over twenty years earlier and commemorated those who had lost their lives in the attempt to reach a safer place. The plaque was placed amongst others marking the refugee story of Australians of Slovenian, Jewish, Serbian, Ukrainian, Polish, Estonian, Latvian, Lithuanian and Tatar background.

In 1997, in a park in Auburn, a Sydney suburb, members of the local Turkish community planted a pine tree grown from a seed from Lone Pine at Anzac Cove on the Gallipoli Peninsula, Turkey. That was the place where Australia first went to war as a nation in the Great War of 1914-18. The planting ceremony acknowledged the common history shared at the beginning of the century when Turkish and Australian soldiers faced each other in battle.

Happy anniversary

Anniversaries associated with the immigrant experience have become commonplace in Australia. Fiftieth anniversaries were particularly popular as the century closed, fifty years on from the mass migration program of the 1950s.

In 1992 the 'Dunera Boys' held a reunion in Melbourne, fifty years after their arrival in Australia as refugees from Hitler's Germany.

'If our example is at all typical, it suggests that what are widely regarded as undesirables at one time later usually become normal and useful citizens of the country admitting them and often, highly regarded members of society.'

Professor Fred Gruen, speaking at the 50th anniversary of the arrival of the *Dunera*

THE CHANGING FACE OF AUSTRALIA

These eight Australian citizens, each one from a different country, were part of a gathering to celebrate the 50th anniversary of Australian citizenship in 1999. 2.8 million residents took up citizenship between Australia Day in 1949, when the first citizenship ceremony was held in Canberra, and 31 December 1995.

Most refugees had become Australian citizens, as had a very high proportion of post-war European settlers. Those who came from English-speaking countries, mostly British-born and New Zealand-born residents, showed least interest in taking up citizenship.

In 1999 South Australia's Tatar-Bashkurt community marked fifty years of the presence of Tatars in Australia. They met with the Minister for Immigration, Philip Ruddock (centre), presenting him with a Tatar cap. Standing on his left was Mahira Hayretdinova-Nadolny who was the first to come, in 1949, having survived forced labour in Germany during the war.

In August 1999 Lyall Fricker (centre), the first Adult Migrant English Program teacher in Adelaide, was reunited with his first students, Galdino (left) and Duilo Caon, at 50th anniversary celebrations organised by the English Language and Literacy Services of the Adelaide Institute of TAFE.

Taking a stand: the Republic

On 6 November 1999 Australians voted in a referendum to decide whether Australia would become a Republic with an Australian Head of State. The majority of Australians in a majority of states voted to remain a constitutional Monarchy with Queen Elizabeth II as Australia's Head of State. A large proportion of the No vote, however, had rejected the Republican model that was proposed rather than approved of the continuing role of the Queen as Head of State.

Like many Australians with an immigrant background, this cross-section of South Australians, attending an Australian Republican Movement dinner in August 1999, supported the move for an Australian Republic. They represented the argument that a republic and an Australian Head of State would be appropriate for Australia as a culturally diverse nation which, at the end of the 20th century, had fewer social and emotional ties to Britain, the 'Old Country'. On the other hand, other overseas-born Australians voted No in the referendum. Some, having come from countries with unstable or autocratic Republican systems of government, feared the impact that a Republic might have had on Australia's democracy. Voting patterns were complex and place of birth was only one factor determining the way Australians voted.

Taking a stand: Reconciliation

In the late 1990s, ethnic organisations responded to the opportunity for reconciliation with Indigenous Australians who had been dispossessed of their traditional lands by two centuries of immigration. Reconciliation acknowledged their unique status as Australia's First Peoples, the 'original owners and custodians of traditional lands and waters'.

When Morris Mansour, President of the African Communities Council in New South Wales, stood with Evelyn Scott, Chairperson of the Council for Aboriginal Reconciliation, in June 1999 they held together the Draft Document for Reconciliation. A statement of intent for action in the future.

Next spread: In the 1990s, reconciliation between Indigenous and immigrant Australians began to take place at the grass roots level in communities across Australia. In 1995 a group of women from the Migrant Resource Centre in Alice Springs spent a day singing, dancing and cooking with students from the local Institute for Aboriginal Development.

One People, One Destiny

It is fitting to end this story of immigration to Australia in the 20th century with the Principles of Multiculturalism from the 1989 National Agenda for a Multicultural Australia. In 1995 the National Multicultural Advisory Council reaffirmed these Principles as 'the framework for the Australia of the twenty-first century'.

The 1989 National Agenda for a Multicultural Australia Principles of Multiculturalism.

1   *All Australians should have a commitment to Australia and share responsibility for furthering our national interests.*

2   *All Australians should be able to enjoy the basic right of freedom from discrimination on the basis of race, ethnicity, religion or culture.*

3   *All Australians should enjoy equal life chances and have equitable access to and an equitable share of the resources which governments manage on behalf of the community.*

4   *All Australians should have the opportunity to participate in society and in the decisions which directly affect them.*

5   *All Australians should be able to develop and make use of their potential for Australia's economic and social development.*

6   *All Australians should have the opportunity to acquire and develop proficiency in English and languages other than English, and to develop cross-cultural understanding.*

7   *All Australians should be able to develop and share their cultural heritage.*

8   *Australian institutions should acknowledge, reflect and respond to the cultural diversity of the Australian community.*

The photographs: sources

The photographs are listed according to the page on which they appear and in the order in which they appear, from top to bottom of the page.

The name of the photographer is listed where known. The catalogue number is also listed where applicable.

If the photograph is adequately described in the extended captions in the text of the book, only the source of the photograph is listed below. Otherwise, the caption is included.

Many of the photographs from the Migration Museum's photographic collection have been copied from privately-held albums. The names of these clubs, families and individuals are listed if this is a requirement of the permission granted to reproduce the image.

All efforts were made to obtain the permission of copyright owners. The Migration Museum, however, will be happy to negotiate with any copyright owners who come forward on an appropriate acknowledgment for any future editions.

1901: A New Nation

12/13
Bicentennial Copying Project, State Library of New South Wales 06773

14
National Library of Australia 16326

15
Battye Library of Western Australian History 9936P; 5323B/1709

History Trust of South Australia Coll PN 874

16/17
Australian Natives' Association Military Ball at Boulder (WA), c1908
Battye Library of Western Australian History 7633B

18
South Australian Museum AA676 AP4464 M Angas collection

19
National Library of Australia 16182

20
Migration Museum/copied from Barossa Valley Archives and Historical Trust 02726

21
John Oxley Library, State Library of Queensland 36195

Hunters Hill Historical Society

22
Chinese procession and the Chinese Citizens' Archway, Swanston St, Melbourne (Vic), during the commemoration of the Duke of York's visit to open the first Australian parliament, 1901
La Trobe Picture Collection, State Library of Victoria, Rose's Stereoscopic Views No 2862 915553

23
John Oxley Library, State Library of Queensland 36390

Hindu workers cutting cane at South Kolan near Bundaberg (Qld), 1904-6
National Library of Australia Greenwood Gillstrom collection

24
Kanakas, Mackay (Qld), c1870s
John Oxley Library, State Library of Queensland 21683

25
Battye Library of Western Australian History 77212P

26
Khyat family outside their store in Exhibition Street, Melbourne, c1904
La Trobe Picture Collection, State Library of Victoria 828458

27
Battye Library of Western Australian History 66659P

1900s - 1910s: One People

28/29
Opening of first Federal parliament, Exhibition Building, Melbourne (Vic), 9 May 1901
National Library of Australia 16314 Album 323/23

30
Immigration promotion poster
National Library of Australia, Parliamentary Papers 1913 vol 2 p 1211

Migrants at Fremantle (WA), c1911
Battye Library of Western Australian History 3051B/206 Courtesy WA Newspapers

31
Denmark Historical Society

32
Types of 'New Chums' – importations of the British Immigration League, Glebe, Sydney (NSW), 'The Sun' 6 July, 1913.
Taken from a copy held in the State Library of New South Wales BN483

Immigrants for New South Wales. Group of farm workers ready to embark, England (?), May 1910
Government Printing Office collection, State Library of New South Wales 11970

33
*Female immigrants,
recruited as domestics
outside their hostel in
Norwood, Adelaide (SA),
c1913*
History Trust of South
Australia, Glass Negatives
Collection

*House of J G Gomme, new
settler, arrived from Isle of
Wight on ss Omrah, 1905,
Bridgetown (WA), 1907*
Battye Library of Western
Australian History 20810P

34
*Empire Settlers; 'we are all
satisfied with Tasmania'.
Some of the new settlers in
the Tamar country. In this
group Great Britain, South
Africa and India are
represented.
Photographed at a show in
the Tamar Valley (Tas),
'Weekly Courier' 17 April
1913*
State Library of Tasmania

35
Government Printing Office
collection, State Library of
New South Wales 28737

*View of Melbourne (Vic),
showing Flinders St (birds
eye vie looking towards
factories on the other side
of the river), c1905-28*
La Trobe Picture
Collection, State Library of
Victoria 781839

36
*Maltese labourers on a
road gang at Mt Lyell
copper mine (Tas), c1913*
Dr Barry York

37
*Mick Kanis' first business in
Australia – a fruit stall with
his brother John in Perth
(WA), 1910-20*
La Trobe Picture
Collection, State Library of
Victoria 819201

*First Bulgarian settlers in
SA, arrived 1910-13. Photo
taken at Broken Hill (NSW)*
Migration Museum 03738/
courtesy of the Staiff family

38
*'Brisbane Courier' June 8,
1910, p 5*
John Oxley Library, State
Library of Queensland
31175

*De Angelis grocery
business, Prahran, Victoria,
1911*
Italian Historical Society
CO.AS.IT, Victoria 11/2
Entry 318

39
*'Queenslander' 6 January
1912*
John Oxley Library, State
Library of Queensland
10106

Jewish Museum of
Australia B30995-25

40
*William Ah Ket, Melbourne
(Vic), 1912*
Chinese Families
collection, Chinese
Museum of Australia

41
From 'Alien Edwardians'
National Archives of
Australia

42
National Archives of
Australia CA 785 ST84/1
Item No 1908/477 2196

43
From 'Alien Edwardians'
National Archives of
Australia

44/45
Chinese Families
collection, Chinese
Museum of Australia

46
*Soon Lee laundry, Hay St,
Perth(WA), c1900*
Battye Library of Western
Australian History 76902P

*Poon Num outside his
family home, Rose Park,
Adelaide (SA), 1913-15*
Migration Museum 03315/
courtesy of Richard Num

47
John Oxley Library, State
Library of Queensland
16956

*Kanakas mustered at
Cairns (Qld) courthouse
prior to repatriation. 1st
shipment under
Commonwealth Act. 3
November 1906*
John Oxley Library, State
Library of Queensland
30243

48
*A Kanaka home in the
Farleigh District, Mackay
(Qld), 'North Queensland
Register', November 23,
1908*
John Oxley Library, State
Library of Queensland
18059

*Finnish sugar workers,
Elphistan Pocket, Ingham
(Qld), 1911*
John Oxley Library, State
Library of Queensland
24641

49
*Spanish immigrants from
the Province of Catalonia
that arrived by the Bulow
in Sydney last week, The
Australasian, July 13, 1907*
National Library of
Australia

50
Battye Library of Western
Australian History 2240B/4

51
*'North Queensland
Register', 5 March 1906*
John Oxley Library, State
Library of Queensland
60932

52
Battye Library of Western
Australian History 7615B

*Queensland Irish
Association hurling team,
1915*
John Oxley Library, State
Library of Queensland
36136

53
*English in Queensland,
possibly Gympie, c1916*
John Oxley Library, State
Library of Queensland
12660

*Seven Hills East school,
Polish Hill River (SA), 1915*
Migration Museum 00542

54
John Oxley Library, State
Library of Queensland
49925

Battye Library of Western
Australian History 76900P

55
*Aboriginals at a corroboree
(WA), c1909. Charlie Crow
in centre and wife in front.*
Battye Library of Western
Australian History 7758B

Lutheran Archives

56
Migration Museum 00797

*Scandinavian masquerade
ball, South Brisbane Town
Hall, Queensland, c1906*
John Oxley Library, State
Library of Queensland
41521

57
*Italians who attended
Melbourne Fruiterers' 1st
annual picnic, Sorrento,
Victoria, 1906*
Italian Historical Society,
CO.AS.IT, 6/2 Entry no:
1539

*The immigrants first
Christmas in Queensland,
News-Budget 23
December 1911*
John Oxley Library, State
Library of Queensland
153342

1914 - 1918

Australians at War

58/59
Princes Hill Primary School

60
Wongarbon (NSW) war memorial, Anzac Day, 1921
La Trobe Picture Collection, State Library of Victoria 734736

61
First Expeditionary Force marching to camp, Melbourne 1914
La Trobe Picture Collection, State Library of Victoria 738493

62
La Trobe Picture Collection, State Library of Victoria 780137

63
Private Mack, South Australia, c1914-18
South Australian Museum

64
Chinese Families collection Chinese Museum of Australia

65
Lutheran Archives

66
Concentration camp for German civil prisoners-of-war, 1914-15
Mortlock Library of South Australiana, State Library of South Australia B12161

67
Toilet facilities, Torrens Island (SA), 1915
Photographer Paul Dubotzki State Library of New South Wales MLMSS261/2 Item 17

Internees dressed as court ladies and jester for the Kaiser's birthday, Torrens Island, 27 January 1915
Photographer Paul Dubotzki State Library of New South Wales MLMSS 261/2 Item 17

68
Lutheran Archives 04464

69
Ambleside Post Office, formerly and currently the Hahndorf Post Office, Hahndorf (SA), 1933
Mortlock Library of South Australiana, State Library of South Australia B8902

70
John Oxley Library, State Library of Queensland 20708

71
Mick Mangos in Perth with a friend before he went to Kalgoorlie which he had to leave after the race riots of 1916
La Trobe Picture Collection, State Library of Victoria 819205

1920s - 1930s

Grim Times

72/73
Courtesy of the Huxley family

74
Immigration promotion poster, The call of the stars to British men and women
National Archives of Australia 434/1 1949/3/21685

Skilled workers and their families on their arrival from England to work at Paton & Baldwin's knitting mills, Launceston (Tas), Weekly Courier 21 June 1923
State Library of Tasmania

75
Denmark Historical Society

New arrivals from Great Britain in front of the Queensland Tourist Office, Sydney, 1926
John Oxley Library, State Library of Queensland 64339

76
British women migrants 1920s
National Library of Australia. Photograph from London News Agency

77
Migration Museum 04357

Widowed domestics and children arrive, post World War I, Sydney (NSW)
Government Printing Office collection, State Library of New South Wales 30415

78
Children from Dr Barnardo's Home arriving to settle, 1924
National Library of Australia

79
Arrival of boy immigrants for South Australia, 1922 The Advertiser June 1922

His Excellency, the Governor of South Australia, Sir George Bridges, visiting Hermannsburg school, Northern Territory, 1 July 1923
AIATSIS/courtesy of Lutheran Archives

80
Frank Manicola's passport photograph, Malta, 1924
La Trobe Picture Collection, State Library of Victoria 832880

Migration Museum 03880/courtesy of Molinara Sports and Social Club

81
Italian Historical Society, CO.AS.IT, 35-63 Entry 1668

Migration Museum 00772

82
Migration Museum 03858/courtesy of Molinara Sports and Social Club

Evan Kiosses and Tanas Radis working at Watson Quarries near Cungena, Eyre Peninsula (SA), 1937
Migration Museum 04052

83
Italian Historical Society, CO.AS.IT.

Workers, mostly Italian, building a road bridge at Ballan near Ballarat (Vic), 1928
Italian Historical Society, CO.AS.IT, 37/4 Entry 109

84
Migration Museum 03292/courtesy of History Trust of South Australia

85
Migration Museum 00134

Innisfail and District Historical Society Inc

86
Jewish Museum of Australia

Italian Historical Society, CO.AS.IT, 37/33 Entry 1733

87
John Oxley Library, State Library of Queensland 60934

Richmond River Historical Society

88
Local History Unit, Mona Vale Public Library/ Courtesy of Matt Slavich

89
Staiff and Doceff families on their market garden, Murray Bridge (SA), 1920
Migration Museum 03737

John Oxley Library, State Library of Queensland/ Courtesy of Mary Scalora, Dante Alighieri Society of Stanthorpe

90
Italian Historical Society, CO.AS.IT, 31/11 Entry 1227

John Oxley Library, State Library of Queensland 41452

91
Battye Library of Western Australian History 27075P

Bicentennial Copying Project, State Library of New South Wales 03552

92
Assisting diver onto ship, Broome (WA), 1938
Battye Library of Western· Australian History 816B/B5654

Japanese cemetery, Broome (WA), 1938
Battye Library of Western Australian History 816B/B5637

93
Indentured crew leaving for home, Broome (WA), 1931
Battye Library of Western Australian History 27257P

Fishermen and agents on the wharves, many of whom are from Molfetta, Port Pirie (SA), 1930s
Migration Museum 03335/Corporation of the City of Port Pirie

Jewish orchardists, Shepparton (Vic), 1920s
Jewish Museum of Australia B30995-37

94
Immigrants hostel, Fremantle, c1920
Battye Library of Western Australian History 5125B

95
Tree felling, Denmark (WA) Group Settlement Scheme, 1920s
Denmark Historical Society

Tin shacks, Busselton (WA), c1920s
Busselton Historical Society

Southall farm, Group settlement 105, Kentdale area near Denmark (WA), 1924
Denmark Historical Society

96
McLeod Creek temporary school, Augusta (WA), 1926
Augusta Historical Museum

Vehicle on boggy road, Augusta (WA), 1926
Augusta Historical Museum

97
Farming cabbages, Ould farm on Group settlement 116, Denmark (WA), 1920s
Denmark Historical Society

The Great Southern Co-operative Butter Company, Denmark (WA), late 1920s
Denmark Historical Society

98
Bruce's Army: Labor electoral poster, 1928
National Library of Australia Theodore Papers MS 7222

99
Mr and Mrs Spano in their first fruit shop at 119 Union Road, Ascot Vale, Melbourne, 1935. The shop was operating since 1926.
Italian Historical Society, CO.AS.IT. 35/52 Entry 1327

100
All images: Battye Library of Western Australian History

101
Migration Museum 04050

Argyle Gardens, Carlton (Vic), 1932
Italian Historical Society, CO.AS.IT.

102
Italian Historical Society, CO.AS.IT. 34/14 Entry 331

103
John Oxley Library, State Library of Queensland 105120

Freeleagus family, taken in front of Phaleiron, Stanley Street, South Brisbane (Qld), 1925
John Oxley Library, State Library of Queensland 50136

Members of the Greek Orthodox Church at opening of the first Greek Orthodox church in Charlotte Street, Brisbane (Qld), 1929
John Oxley Library, State Library of Queensland 62014

104
Chinese Families collection Chinese Museum of Australia

105
Coronation festivities of Edward VIII, Brisbane (Qld), Courier Mail 13 May 1937 p17
John Oxley Library, State Library of Queensland 20710

Presentation at Kanis's cafe by Richmond Football Club of the Best and Fairest Trophy donated annually by Mick Kanis, Bridge Road, Richmond (Vic), 1930s
La Trobe Picture Collection, State Library of Victoria 819101

Hindmarsh British Football Club, Adelaide (SA), 1923
Migration Museum 03442

106
Playing traditional Italian instruments, Riverland (SA), 1930s
Migration Museum 04303

Italian Historical Society, CO.AS.IT./*The Australian Musical News*

107
Background: Welsh flag flying above David Jones department store on St David's Day, the Welsh National Day, Sydney (NSW), c1930s
Hood Collection, State Library of New South Wales 14101

Scottish mother and daughter at Highland gathering, Sydney (NSW), c1930s
Hood Collection, State Library of New South Wales 01450

Chinese Families collection, Chinese Museum of Australia

108
Hood Collection, State Library of New South Wales 20358

Boys from St Patrick's School, St Patrick's Day, South Perth Zoological and Botanical Gardens (WA), 1929
Battye Library of Western Australian History 3699B/13/168

Interior of Langmeil Lutheran church decorated for confirmation, Tanunda (SA), c1920s-30s
Lutheran Archives 01640

109
Outdoor picture theatre, Broome (WA), 1920
Battye Library of Western Australian History 53225P

110
Passport of Edna Sara Lebmann, signed in Germany and in Australia, 1939
Jewish Museum of Australia 392.5

111
Dr Steven Kinston
Musica Viva Australia/Courtesy of Warren Kinston

112/113

Albert Que Noy in uniform, c1939-45
Chinese Museum of Darwin Chung Wah Historical Collection/courtesy of Frank Que Noy

114

Spiro Polites in the Labour Corps, Tocumwal (Vic), 1942-3
La Trobe Picture Collection, State Library of Victoria 818249

Frederick Darwish Malouf, son of Darwish, in the army, 1942
La Trobe Picture Collection, State Library of Victoria 829324

115

Nellie Fong with rotary hoe at Nellie and Thomas Fong's market garden, Pine Creek (NT), 1943
Chinese Museum of Darwin Chung Wah Historical Collection/ Courtesy of Joan Fong

Aboriginal soldiers in uniform, c1939-45
Australian Institute for Aboriginal and Torres Strait Islander Studies (AIATSIS)

116

Chinese collect for China Relief Fund, Brisbane (Qld), 'Courier Mail', 1942
John Oxley Library, State Library of Queensland 62477

Fundraising for the Greek war effort, Melbourne (Vic), c1939-45
La Trobe Picture Collection, State Library of Victoria 817926

117

Anzac Day, Berrigan (NSW), 25 April 1940
La Trobe Picture Collection, State Library of Victoria 818321

Nicolangelo Turci with his cousin Genaro Turci, Molfettese fishermen, Port Pirie (SA), 1948
Migration Museum 03269

118

Italian Historical Society, CO.AS.IT. 27-6 Entry No 92

Hood Collection, State Library of New South Wales 07963

119

ID photograph for Italian internee, Stefano Stefani, 1941
Courtesy of Julian Stefani

Italian internees being moved out of Compound 9, Loveday (SA), 1943
Hedley Cullen photographer
Migration Museum 01203

120

Migration Museum 04302

Migration Museum 04308

121

Japanese internees on a working party to fell timber at Woolenook, River Murray near Renmark (SA), c1943
Hedley Cullen photographer
Migration Museum 01186

122

Prisoner-of-war camp, Cowra (NSW), mid 1940s
Italian Historical Society, CO.AS.IT.

123

Both images: *Italian prisoners-of-war at work on Bartlett family banana farm, Middle Pocket (NSW), mid 1940s*
Italian Historical Society, CO.AS.IT.

124

German internees arrive by the ship Dunera at Pyrmont (NSW) on the 6th of September 1940
Photographer F J Halmarick *The Sydney Morning Herald*/Fairfax Photo Library 46223

125

Displaced Persons Camp in Germany, c1946
A United Nations photograph, Migration Museum 00443

126

Migration Museum 03740

127

Migration Museum 02378

Migration Museum 03931

128

Franciszek Samojlowicz in shoemakers' workshop, Fallingbostel DP camp, Germany 1946-47
Migration Museum 03742

Students enrolled at Brunschweig Technical School, Germany, late 1940s
Migration Museum 00254

129

Concentration camp victims at end of war, Europe, c1945
Jewish Museum of Australia 1392.16

130

Migration Museum 00083

Polish Carpathian brigade, Palestine, 1940
Migration Museum 03284

131

Neptuna burning after first bombing raid by Japanese bombers on Darwin (NT), February 1942.
Museum and Art Gallery of the Northern Territory, Canniford Collection, PIC032/040

132/3

Department of Immigration and Multicultural Affairs 47/4A/4 (4340)

134

Department of Immigration and Multicultural Affairs 47/3/6 (2)

Department of Immigration and Multicultural Affairs 50/51A/1 (4367)

135

Jewish Museum of Australia

136

Lithuanian Displaced Persons ready to leave for Australia, West Germany, late 1940s
Courtesy of Martin Deckys

137

The Sziller family travelling by train from West Germany to Italy prior to departure for Australia, c1949
Migration Museum 03958

138

Displaced Persons on their way to Australia, late 1940s
Migration Museum 00249

139

Department of Immigration and Multicultural Affairs 62/32/4

Department of Immigration and Multicultural Affairs 56/4/1 (316)

140
*Background: Running
along the beach*
National Archives of
Australia A1200
L13187/Commonwealth of
Australia copyright
reproduced by permission

*Enquiry counter, Australia
House, London, 1962*
Department of Immigration
and Multicultural Affairs
62/14/19 (1474)

141
*Promotion of the Bring Out
A Briton scheme in the
Good Neighbour bulletin,
No 53, June 1958*
Department of Immigration
and Multicultural Affairs

142
Department of Immigration
and Multicultural Affairs
Photographer Don
Edwards 58/7/20 (703)

*On January 22, 1962, 24
British migrant families
arrived at Fremantle (WA)
in the liner Canberra*
Department of Immigration
and Multicultural Affairs
62/7/20 (1441)

143
Department of Immigration
and Multicultural Affairs
67/4/3 (2298)

Department of Immigration
and Multicultural Affairs
Photographer Don
Edwards 59/4/46 (890)

144/5
*The Lester family prior to
their departure for
Australia, Hornchurch,
Essex, England, 1964*
Courtesy of Leslie and
Joyce Lester

*Leslie and Joyce Lester,
Melbourne (Vic), 1996*
Photographer Kate Walsh
Migration Museum

146
*Roman Catholic children-
girls; arrival of immigrants
via 'Asturias', Fremantle
(WA), 22 September 1947*
Battye Library of Western
Australian History
816B/C1252

Department of Immigration
and Multicultural Affairs
64/8/1 (1792)

147
*Hedley Caffyn, Mrs Caffyn
and children, Colin 6, and
Jennifer, 3 - are all 'second
timers'. Good Neighbour
bulletin, May 1955*
Department of Immigration
and Multicultural Affairs

*Mrs Nora Brookes, of
Warlingham (centre)
pictured on her reunion
with her daughter Clare
Oliver and grand children,
Julie, Nicholas, Susan and
Annette, Perth (WA), 1968*
Department of Immigration
and Multicultural Affairs
68/34/34 (2845)

148
*Migrant processing -
Germany, 1956*
Department of Immigration
and Multicultural Affairs
56/14/69

149
Department of Immigration
and Multicultural Affairs
55/4/114 (220)

*People at a wharf in Italy
farewelling family and
friends leaving for
Australia, c1960s*
Migration Museum 03075/
reproduced with the
permission of FILEF

150
*ICEM arrivals by Qantas
Britannia aircraft (Belgians),
1962*
Department of Immigration
and Multicultural Affairs
62/4/66 (1418)

151
Migration Museum
03187/courtesy of the
Spinelli family

152
*Seventy-five Greek girl
domestics flew into
Melbourne in two airlifts
from Athens late last
month (June). Immigration
officials make
arrangements to transport
them to Maribyrnong
Hostel, Melbourne, where
they stay two or three days
before starting work in
Melbourne homes, 1962*
Department of Immigration
and Multicultural Affairs
62/4/80 (1422)

153
Department of Immigration
and Multicultural Affairs
60/4/7 (1073)

154
Department of Immigration
and Multicultural Affairs
56/4/37 (325)

155
Migration Museum
SL00109

Migration Museum
SL00122

156
Migration Museum 03385

157
*Three generations of
women and children on
their way to be reunited
with husbands and fathers
already in Australia,
c1950s-60s*
Migration Museum
03842/Molinara Social and
Sports Club Inc

158
*Reunion of Mrs Ferraro and
her five sons, Adelaide,
1951*
Migration Museum 00130/
courtesy of The Advertiser,
from The News, 3 May
1951

159
*Migrant children enjoy the
facilities of the children's
playroom aboard the
Fairsky under the eye of
trained sisters, 1962*
Department of Immigration
and Multicultural Affairs
62/4/30 (1409)

*Fancy dress party on the
'Fairsea, 1964*
Leslie and Joyce Lester

160
*Dinner party on board ship
to Australia*
Migration Museum 04311

La Trobe Picture
Collection, State Library of
Victoria 833237

161
La Trobe Picture
Collection, State Library of
Victoria 833283

162
Department of Immigration
and Multicultural Affairs
54/4/13 (104)

Department of Immigration
and Multicultural Affairs
Photographer Don
Edwards 55/4/36 (198)

163
*The 'Good Neighbour'
bulletin No 131, December
1964*
Department of Immigration
and Multicultural Affairs

Department of Immigration
and Multicultural Affairs
63/4/2 (1583)

164
Department of Immigration
and Multicultural Affairs
53/22/5 (95)

*Bonegilla (NSW) Migrant
Reception Centre, Block
No 18*
Photographer W Koslovski
Migration Museum 01536

165
Migration Museum 01853

Government Printing Office
collection, State Library of
New South Wales 50374

166
Courtesy of Derek and
Shirley Taylor

*Laundry facilities, Bonegilla
Migrant Reception Centre,
Albury (NSW), 1949*
Department of Immigration
and Multicultural Affairs
49/22/17

167
Courtesy of Derek and
Shirley Taylor

Department of Immigration
and Multicultural Affairs
57/22/31 (620)

168
Courtesy of Peter Cahalan

*John Maxwell and his
family outside their
suburban home, 1953*
Photographer J Tanner
National Archives of
Australia A1200
L15691/Commonwealth of
Australia copyright
reproduced by permission

169
Department of Immigration
and Multicultural Affairs
65/22/7 (2059)

*'Good Neighbour bulletin',
No 181, February 1969*
Department of Immigration
and Multicultural Affairs

170
*Displaced Persons at the
Hume Weir, near Albury
(NSW), December 1947*
Department of Immigration
and Multicultural Affairs
47/3/7 (2)

Migration Museum 04380

171
Migration Museum 03965

Department of Immigration
and Multicultural Affairs

172
Department of Immigration
and Multicultural Affairs
54/22/18c (172)

*Migrant children at Wacol
centre, near Brisbane, each
get a bottle of free milk,
1957*
Department of Immigration
and Multicultural Affairs
Photographer Don
Edwards 57/22/27 (619)

173
Migration Museum 01857

174/5
Migration Museum/
courtesy of Rosa Garcia

176
Department of Immigration
and Multicultural Affairs
53/8/11 (64)

*Interior of the dormitory,
Fairbridge Farm (WA)*
Battye Library of Western
Australian History
816B/C2580

177
Australian Institute for
Aboriginal and Torres Strait
Islander Studies 1609.12

178
Department of Immigration
and Multicultural Affairs
68/4/26 (2525)

179
Australian Photographic
Agency Collection, State
Library of New South
Wales 02621

180
Australian Photographic
Agency Collection, State
Library of New South
Wales 20277

181
Migration Museum
03807/courtesy of Robert
Nicholl

*Army captain Nerig Hwan
Wang, Melbourne, c1943*
Chinese Families collection
Chinese Museum of
Australia

182
*Kumi Fuzioka, in a
traditional wedding
kimono, for her marriage
to Australian soldier,
Maxwell Barnes, Japan,
late 1940s-early 1950s*
Courtesy of Kumi Barnes

*Max and Kumi Barnes and
their daughter, Tasmania,
mid 1950s*
Courtesy of Kumi Barnes

183
City of Belmont Historical
Society/courtesy of
Jeannette Antoinette

National Library of
Australia 21027
Photographer Wolfgang
Sievers

184
Australian Institute for
Aboriginal and Torres Strait
Islander Studies 4612.12/
reproduced with the
permission of *Canberra
Times*

185
*Italian Displaced Person,
Alfredo Floramo, working
at a timber mill, Manjimup,
Western Australia, 1950*
Migration Museum
03102/courtesy of Alfredo
Floramo

*Polish Displaced Persons
working on the Hydro-
Electric Scheme, Butlers
Gorge, Tasmania, 1950*
Migration Museum 00349

186
*Polish Displaced Persons
building a railway line from
Penong to a gypsum mine
at Kowulka on the far west
coast of South Australia,
1949*
Migration Museum 03763

*Tent accommodation for
Displaced Persons working
for the South Australian
Railways, Adelaide, early
1950s*
Migration Museum
03924/courtesy of
TransAdelaide archives

187
*Displaced Persons working
as kitchen staff, Woodside
migrant hostel (SA), c1949-
52*
Migration Museum 03968

*Polish Displaced Person,
Eudoxia Rakowski with
friend, picking grapes,
Renmark (SA), 1949*
Migration Museum 01545

188
*Andreas Dezsery when he
established his cleaning
company, Adelaide (SA),
1953*
Migration Museum 04122

189
*Mr and Mrs Rakowski with
staff outside their
delicatessen, Port Adelaide
(SA), 1955*
Migration Museum 01568

Department of Immigration
and Multicultural Affairs
62/13/10 (1465)

190
*Tunnel workers on the
Snowy Mountains Scheme,
Tooma-Tumut tunnel
(NSW), 1960*
Department of Immigration
and Multicultural Affairs
60/16/54

191
*Russian Displaced Person,
Kiril Makeyev, working as a
surveyor on the Snowy
Mountains Scheme,
Jindabyne, 1950*
Migration Museum 04114

*Alexander Makeyev and his
first Australian snowman,
New Jindabyne, 1955*
Migration Museum 04120

192
*German workers on the
Snowy Mountains Scheme,
early 1950s, from the
'Good Neighbour' bulletin,
March 1967*
Department of Immigration
and Multicultural Affairs

*Joachim Hasse (right) and
friends on the banks of the
River Torrens, Adelaide
(SA), 1951*
Migration Museum 04320

193
*Port Kembla steelworks
(NSW), 1955*
Department of Immigration
and Multicultural Affairs
55/16/74 (261)

*Carpenters at work forming
a concrete inlet tower in a
filtration tank at Western
Creek sewerage project,
Canberra (ACT), 1957*
Department of Immigration
and Multicultural Affairs
57/16/10 (580)

194
*Two British migrant
bricklayers work on a new
house at Elizabeth, South
Australia, 1958*
Department of Immigration
and Multicultural Affairs
Photographer Don
Edwards 58/10/19

*Migrant and Australian
shipyard workers on the
foredeck of Iron Flinders,
Whyalla (SA), 1958*
Department of Immigration
and Multicultural Affairs
Photographer Don
Edwards 58/16/268 (814)

195
Department of Immigration
and Multicultural Affairs
57/22/32 (620)

196
Department of Immigration
and Multicultural Affairs
55/16/12a (245)

*Alumina section at Bell
Bay, Australian and new
settler fitters (Tas), 1958*
Department of Immigration
and Multicultural Affairs
Photographer Don
Edwards 58/16/19 (752)

197
Department of Immigration
and Multicultural Affairs
66/16/50 (2211)

198

Romano Rubichi with some of his Australian pupils at the Modbury Primary School, Adelaide (SA), 1966
Department of Immigration and Multicultural Affairs
66/29/6 (2270)

Felicity Rhodes (right) with a young mod customer in her Australian boutique, Geraldton (WA), 1969
Department of Immigration and Multicultural Affairs
69/16/651 (3120)

Fred Witsenhuysen, sub-editor of Adelaide News (Dutch), 1957
Department of Immigration and Multicultural Affairs
57/16/27

199

Department of Immigration and Multicultural Affairs
57/16/28 (584)

Department of Immigration and Multicultural Affairs
69/29/43 (3294)

200

Department of Immigration and Multicultural Affairs
55/4/92 (214)

Migration Museum 03928

201

Stockmen on the Hermannsburg run, Northern Territory, 1950s
Australian Institute for Aboriginal and Torres Strait Islander Studies 6481.02

Department of Immigration and Multicultural Affairs
66/16/92 (2222)

Department of Immigration and Multicultural Affairs
66/2/26 (2157)

202

Department of Immigration and Multicultural Affairs
54/16/23 (148)

Mr Gerhard May, in charge of construction of the complicated arch rib supports for the roof, came to Australia five years ago, Opera House construction site, Sydney (NSW), 1964
Department of Immigration and Multicultural Affairs
64/16/22 (1818)

203

Elizabeth Quinn, formerly of Belfast (Ireland) at the steel plate machine, Newcastle (NSW), 1954)
Department of Immigration and Multicultural Affairs
54/16/22 (148)

English nursing sister at Canberra Hospital (ACT), 1969
Department of Immigration and Multicultural Affairs
69/29/42 (3293)

204

Pat O'Neill at her ledger machine, Adelaide (SA), 1964
Department of Immigration and Multicultural Affairs
64/16/23 (1821)

Department of Immigration and Multicultural Affairs
59/14/2 (931)

205

Gemilio Sagazio puts the finishing touches to a motel swimming pool, Darwin (NT), 1967
Department of Immigration and Multicultural Affairs
67/16/58 (2343)

Local Studies Unit, Mona Vale Library/courtesy Berta Cunico

206

Italian Historical Society, CO.AS.IT.

Department of Immigration and Multicultural Affairs
70/16/78 (3428)

207

Kazmer Ujvari, pastrycook, in his business Budapest Cakes, Adelaide (SA), 1950s
Courtesy of Kazzy Ujvari

Italian Historical Society, CO.AS.IT.

208

Department of Immigration and Multicultural Affairs
69/16/409 (3059)

Poppy having obtained a diploma opened her own business from home. She was possibly the first Greek women's hairdresser in Melbourne, Victoria, 1957
La Trobe Picture Collection, State Library of Victoria 820241

First Spinelli knitting factory, Adelaide, South Australia, 1962
Migration Museum 03180/courtesy of the Spinelli family

209

Greek sponge-fishers leave their island of Kalymnos for Australia, from 'Good Neighbour' bulletin, No 6, June 1954
Department of Immigration and Multicultural Affairs

Nicholas Paspaley senior with a Japanese technician, Darwin, 1950s
Courtesy of Paspaley Pearls

210

Mr de Jager at work on a guitar, (WA), 1962 (Dutch)
Department of Immigration and Multicultural Affairs
62/6/12 (1431)

Aldo Rossi working on the mosaic in the Hall of Memories at the Australian War Memorial, Canberra (ACT), 1955
Department of Immigration and Multicultural Affairs
55/16/16 (246)

211

First house in Australia for the Kapociunas family, Kensington, South Australia, early 1950s
Migration Museum 03796

212

Migration Museum 01874

State Library of New South Wales 05171/reproduced with the permission of Colonial Ltd

213

La Trobe Picture Collection, State Library of Victoria 821659

Houses under construction at Elizabeth, South Australia, 1958
Photographer Don Edwards Department of Immigration and Multicultural Affairs
58/10/12

214

Courtesy of Martin Deckys

215

Migration Museum 03962

Migration Museum 03956

216

Migration Museum 03106/courtesy of Alfredo Floramo

Migration Museum 03747

217

Brisbane Lord Mayor explains significance of crown to migrant children (Qld), 1953
Department of Immigration and Multicultural Affairs
53/17/15 (81)

218

Migration Museum 00355

219

'Good Neighbour' bulletin, No 78, July 1960
Department of Immigration and Multicultural Affairs

Department of Immigration and Multicultural Affairs
61/19/29 (1358)

220

City of Belmont Historical Society/courtesy of the Daws family

The Mesker family returning from a swim, Collaroy (NSW), 1965
Department of Immigration and Multicultural Affairs
65/23/15 (2068)

German immigrants in the backyard of the house rented by Helene and Josef Sandl, Melbourne (Vic), 1961
La Trobe Picture Collection, State Library of Victoria 833290

221

Ukrainian dancers at a Highland gathering at Manuka Oval, Canberra, 1951, from The New Australian, no 36 December 1951
Department of Immigration and Multicultural Affairs

222

Migration Museum 04376

223
From: T Kempa (ed),
The Monument of Polish-
Australian Brotherhood in
Arms, Hobart, Tasmania,
1984
Migration Museum 00315

Migration Museum 04012

224
Swiss prefabricated house
imported to South
Australia, 1965
Department of Immigration
and Multicultural Affairs
65/21/1 (2055)

225
The Chiarolli and Nassig
households preparing
grapes for wine, South
Australia 1958
Migration Museum
03163/courtesy of Maria
Pallotta-Chiarolli

John Oxley Library, State
Library of Queensland/
courtesy of Mary Scalora
and the Orsetto family

226
Presto Smallgoods Factory
in Leichhardt, Sydney, New
South Wales, c1960s
State Library of New South
Wales 22169/copyright
owner unknown

227
Historic Photograph
Collection, MacLeay
Museum, University of
Sydney

John O'Sullivan, licensee
and manager, drinks with
locals in the bar of the
Mellum Club Hotel,
Landsborough (Qld), 1962
Department of Immigration
and Multicultural Affairs
62/13/24 (1469)

228
Dr Mark Siegelberg with
one of his linotypers,
German migrant Paul
Herweg, place unknown
(Aust), 1968
Department of Immigration
and Multicultural Affairs
68/13/64 (2603)

The clubrooms of Savoy
Soccer Club Inc, Port Pirie,
South Australia, 1949
Migration Museum 03266

229
Migration Museum SL
00111

230
Department of Immigration
and Multicultural Affairs
65/17/26 (2039)

231
Department of Immigration
and Multicultural Affairs
65/18/2 (2040)

Courtesy of Australian
Romanian Association

232
Department of Immigration
and Multicultural Affairs
53/18/1 (84)

La Trobe Picture
Collection, State Library of
Victoria 829644

The Donikian family
enjoying a picnic, Lane
Cove National Park,
Sydney, New South Wales,
1950s
Courtesy of George
Donikian

233
Holy Cross Lutheran church
building, a recycled
wartime Nissan hut, to
which builder Mr Gus
Muller had fashioned a
tower
Lutheran Archives 00920

234
Department of Immigration
and Multicultural Affairs
70/17/37 (3517)

Christening at St Nicholas
Orthodox Church,
Yarraville, Melbourne (Vic),
1966
La Trobe Picture
Collection, State Library of
Victoria 819736

235
Wedding party outside St
Christopher's Roman
Catholic Church, Manuka,
Canberra (ACT), 1962
Department of Immigration
and Multicultural Affairs
62/13/8 (1465)

Department of Immigration
and Multicultural Affairs
49/17/4 (9)

236
Department of Immigration
and Multicultural Affairs
68/19/28 (2746)

Department of Immigration
and Multicultural Affairs
68/9/17 (2555)

237
Published on a regular
basis in the 'Good
Neighbour' bulletin, 1950s
Department of Immigration
and Multicultural Affairs

Battye Library of Western
Australian History
816B/C4551

Department of Immigration
and Multicultural Affairs
69/6/95 (2910)

238
Department of Immigration
and Multicultural Affairs
55/12/16 (237)

'Good Neighbour' bulletin,
No 134, March 1965
Department of Immigration
and Multicultural Affairs

239
Chinese Families collection
Chinese Museum of
Australia

240
Department of Immigration
and Multicultural Affairs
65/12/1 (1954)

Department of Immigration
and Multicultural Affairs
59/11/24 (913)

241
Department of Immigration
and Multicultural Affairs
64/13/16 (1809)

242/243
Department of Immigration
and Multicultural Affairs
73/4A/58

244
Sri Lankan son and his
mother, Adelaide, South
Australia, 1987
Department of Immigration
and Multicultural Affairs
87/41A/1

245
Department of Immigration
and Multicultural Affairs
72/29/15 (4143)

Department of Immigration
and Multicultural Affairs
74/16/27 (4282)

246
Courtesy of John Boland

Department of Immigration
and Multicultural Affairs
88/29A/5 (6000)

247
Migration Museum 03806

248
Both images: courtesy of
Alfredo Goldbach and
Sandra de Souza

249
Department of Immigration
and Multicultural Affairs
75/46A/31 (4821)

250

Department of Immigration officer with interpreter My Van Tran interviewing newly arrived Vietnamese refugees, Darwin, Northern Territory, 1977
Department of Immigration and Multicultural Affairs 77/46A/52 (4890)

Department of Immigration officer, Steve Carter, interviewing Indo-Chinese refugees on an island refugee camp, Malaysian peninsula, 1979
Department of Immigration and Multicultural Affairs 79/46A/8 (5022)

251

A group of Indo-Chinese refugees arrives in Canberra (ACT), 1979
Department of Immigration and Multicultural Affairs Photographer John Crowther 79/46A/1 (5019)

252

Migrant hostel residents cooking for themselves, Tamarind Hostel (Qld), 1984
Department of Immigration and Multicultural Affairs C84/22A/405

The Vo family arrive in Hobart, Tasmania, direct from Kuala Lumpur, under the Community Refugee Settlement Scheme, October 1980
Courtesy of *The Mercury*

253

Department of Immigration and Multicultural Affairs 83/46A/15 (5392)

Department of Immigration and Multicultural Affairs 88/46A/1 (6043)

254

Department of Immigration and Multicultural Affairs 83/47A/22 (5400)

255

Iranian Baha'i family, Adelaide (SA), 1984
Courtesy of *The Advertiser* 16 October 1984

Department of Immigration and Multicultural Affairs 84/4A/1 (5403)

256

Courtesy of *The Advertiser* 12 February 1985

257

Department of Immigration and Multicultural Affairs 86/47A/2

Courtesy of Mohamet Beyan. Photographer Hector Farreras

258

Courtesy of Louisa Ferreira

Migration Museum photograph Photographer Kate Walsh

Kosovo Albanians, the Zenuni family, reunited with extended family members in Adelaide, South Australia, 1999
Photographer Darren Seiler Courtesy of *The Advertiser* 22 January 1999

259

Jewish Museum of Australia

Courtesy of the Australian Romanian Association

Courtesy of *The Advertiser* 24 May 1999
Photographer Martin Jacka

260

Courtesy of *The Advertiser* 17 September 1977

Courtesy of John and Marie Boland

261

Department of Immigration and Multicultural Affairs 88/20a/1 (5954)

262

Department of Immigration and Multicultural Affairs 80/48A/103 (5177)

Department of Immigration and Multicultural Affairs 90/46A/6 (6073)

263

Australian National Action 'Sink Them' poster on an Adelaide bus shelter (SA),c1996
Photographer Tiffany Linke Migration Museum SL03090

264

Department of Immigration and Multicultural Affairs 73/25/20 (4244)

Australian Institute for Aboriginal and Torres Strait Islander Studies 5711.289

265

Ethnic Radio presenters, Melbourne (Vic), 1976
Department of Immigration and Multicultural Affairs 76/13A/3 (4823)

Telephone Interpreter Service interpreters, 1982
Department of Immigration and Multicultural Affairs 82/50B/4

266

Department of Immigration and Multicultural Affairs 82/38A/1 (5329)

Department of Immigration and Multicultural Affairs 87/43A/2 (5872)

267

Volunteer with the Good Neighbour Movement (SA), early 1970s
Migration Museum 01933

Italian Group, Botany Migrant Resource Centre, Daceyville (NSW), 1986
Courtesy of Botany Migrant Resource Centre

268

Department of Immigration and Multicultural Affairs 83/42A/1 (5384)

La Trobe Picture Collection, State Library of Victoria 810313

269

Courtesy of Dr Sev Ozdowski

Hon P J Keating, Prime Minister of Australia, talks on seeking a strong national and international identity, 2nd National Immigration Outlook conference, Sydney (NSW) November 1992
Department of Immigration and Multicultural Affairs 92/38B/51

270

Courtesy of Council of Turkish Associations in New South Wales Photographer Cengiz Erginli.

Courtesy of Randolph Alwis, President, FECCA

271

La Trobe Picture Collection, State Library of Victoria Photographer Elizabeth Gilliam 828883

Courtesy of Fairfield Adult Migrant Education Service

272

La Trobe Picture Collection, State Library of Victoria Photographer Elizabeth Gilliam 828854

Migration Museum SL02881 Photographer Kate Walsh

273

An outworker at her machine, Melbourne, Victoria, late 1990s
Photographer Sharon Jones. Courtesy of Textile, Clothing and Footwear Union of Australia

Courtesy of United Trades and Labor Council (SA)

274

A graduation celebration in the Symeonakis family, South Australia, 1970s
Migration Museum 00097

Department of Immigration and Multicultural Affairs 71/16/240 (3811)

275

Battye Library of Western Australian History 89774P

Courtesy of the Vietnamese Association of the Northern Territory

276

Migration Museum SL02885 Photographer Kate Walsh

La Trobe Picture Collection, State Library of Victoria Photographer Emmanuel Santos 830189

277
*Mr Ayoubi and his
daughter in the Miramar
Nut Shop, Brunswick,
Victoria, 1988*
La Trobe Picture
Collection, State Library of
Victoria Photographer
Vivienne Mehes 828524

La Trobe Picture
Collection, State Library of
Victoria Photographer
Elizabeth Gilliam 813277

278
*Victor Liu with spring rolls
ready to be packed, Chien
Wah factory, Clifton Hill,
Melbourne (Vic), 1988*
La Trobe Picture
Collection, State Library of
Victoria Photographer
Emmanuel Santos 808159

*Managing director,
Maurice Crotti, at the San
Remo plant, Windsor
Gardens, Adelaide (SA),
1996*
Photographer Mike Burton
Courtesy of *The Advertiser*,
23 April 1996

279
Department of Immigration
and Multicultural Affairs
71/18/13 (3833)

Courtesy of Mihai
Maghiaru, the Australian
Romanian Association
(NSW)

280
Department of Immigration
and Multicultural Affairs
72/18/39 (4115)

281
*Lieng Hien Asian grocery
store, Adelaide Central
Market (SA), 1995*
Photographer Neale
Winter Migration Museum
SL02893

La Trobe Picture
Collection, State Library of
Victoria Photographer
Dyranda Prevost 821369

282
*Turklstani South
Australians, Sabit and
Habiba Ruzehaji, with a
tandoor oven for making
chapatis and naan bread in
the backyard of their
home, Adelaide, South
Australia, 1995*
Photographer
Aphrodite Vlavogelakis
Migration Museum
SL02851

*Rapid Creek Sunday
markets, Darwin, 1999*
Photographer
Hector Farreras
Courtesy of Chi and
Ratchanee Warawitya

283
Department of Immigration
and Multicultural Affairs
73/9/3 (4197)

Migration Museum 04158

284
Department of Immigration
and Multicultural Affairs
85/13A/2 (5644)

285
Both images: Courtesy of
NSW Auburn Turkish
Islamic Cultural Centre

286
*Lighting the candles in
Fitzroy Gardens before
processing into St Patrick's
Cathedral, Melbourne, for
a service marking the
canonisation of 117
Vietnamese martyrs, 1988*
La Trobe Picture
Collection, State Library of
Victoria Photographer
Emmanuel Santos 810617

287
Department of Immigration
and Multicultural Affairs
88/9A/12 (5891)

288
*Debutantes walking in
procession during the
Blessing of the Fleet
celebrations, Port Pirie,
South Australia, 1988*
Photographer Tony Healy
Migration Museum 02698

*Carrying the statue of Our
Lady of Martyrs from St
Mark's Cathedral, Port
Pirie, South Australia, for
the Blessing of the Fleet
ceremony, 1988*
Photographer Tony Healy
Migration Museum 02658

*The crowd at the end of
Mass at St Anthony's
church, Solomontown, Port
Pirie, South Australia,
during the Blessing of the
Fleet festa, 1988*
Photographer Tony Healy
Migration Museum 02654

289
*The statue of Our Lady of
Martyrs carried on board
the 'Myona' for the
blessing of the waters, Port
Pirie, South Australia, 1988*
Photographer Tony Healy
Migration Museum 02704

290
*Members of the French
community enjoying a
game of petanque,
Adelaide (SA), December
1988*
Courtesy of *The Advertiser*
12 December 1988

Background: *Polonia
Soccer Club junior players,
Adelaide (SA), 1978*
Migration Museum
SL00845

291
*Italian women have made a
sporting breakthrough in
Australia. APIA Club,
Sydney (NSW), 1972*
Department of Immigration
and Multicultural Affairs
72/33/28 (4162)

*Dragon boat in the
Chinese Association of
South Australia dragon
boat racing competition,
Adelaide (SA), 1986*
Migration Museum
SL01802

292/3
Italian Historical Society,
CO.AS.IT./Courtesy of
Il Globo/Bergagna

293
*Finnish Australians at the
Sydney Carnival, New
South Wales, 1988*
Courtesy of Wollongong
District Finnish Society

Courtesy of Brisbane
Migrant Resource Centre

294
Courtesy of the Council of
Turkish Associations in
New South Wales and
Wollongong Turkish
Society Inc
Photographer Cengiz
Erginli

295
Courtesy of the Garcia
family

296
City of Belmont Historical
Society/courtesy of Peg
Parkin

297
Courtesy of the Australian
Romanian Association
(NSW)

298
Courtesy of the African
Communities Council
(NSW)

299
Courtesy of Irek Garipov

300/301
All images: Courtesy of
Mark Pharaoh

302/3
Courtesy of Migrant
Resource Centre of Central
Australia

304
Top left: Courtesy of
Migrant Resource Centre
of Central Australia

Top right: Chinese Families
collection Chinese
Museum of Australia

Courtesy of Josef Gala,
Czechoslovakian
Association of Tasmania

305
Courtesy of Brisbane
Migrant Resource Centre

Courtesy of Morris
Mansour, African
Communities Council
(NSW)

306
Courtesy of Irek Garipov

Courtesy of Ros Paterson,
Cornish Association of
South Australia

307
*Mousbah, Fatima, Bassam
and Jamal Abou-Eid at the
computer in their family
home, Thornbury,
Melbourne (Vic), 1989*
La Trobe Picture
Collection, State Library of
Victoria Photographer
Emmanuel Santos 828237

*Children enjoying a meal
at McDonald's,
Cabramatta, Sydney, New
South Wales, late 1998*
Courtesy of Anglicare
Sydney

308
*An Iranian-born bride with
her groom of German-
Australian background at
their wedding ceremony,
Adelaide, South Australia,
1996*
Photographer
Aphrodite Vlavogelakis
Migration Museum
SL02986

309
Department of Immigration
and Multicultural Affairs
C96/13B/3

310
Chung Wah Historical
Society Courtesy of Adam
Lowe

Migration Museum
photograph

311
Courtesy of the Council of
Turkish Associations in
New South Wales
Photographer Cengiz
Erginli

312
*Reunion of the 'Dunera'
boys, 50 years after their
arrival in Australia, 1992*
Photographer Henry Talbot
National Library of
Australia 19907/
reproduced with the
permission of the estate of
Henry Talbot

313
*Australian citizens from
many different
backgrounds celebrating
the 50th anniversary of
Australian citizenship,
Adelaide Town Hall (SA),
1999*
Photographer Brett
Hartwig
Courtesy of *The Advertiser*,
6 August 1999

Courtesy of Irek Garipov

314
Courtesy of the English
Language and Literacy
Services of the Adelaide
Institute of TAFE

Courtesy of Randolph
Alwis, FECCA

315
Courtesy of Morris
Mansour, African
Communities Council
(NSW)

316/317
Courtesy of Migrant
Resource Centre of Central
Australia

Historical context: sources

Photographs are a source of evidence about the past. Much of the historical information woven around the photographs in *The Changing Face of Australia* was supplied as captions by the museums, archives, libraries, historical societies, newspapers, government agencies, community organisations, families and individuals who participated in this project.

I have also called on a wealth of knowledge built up over a decade as a curator of numerous exhibitions at the Migration Museum.

General information

For historical information, census summaries, and a coverage of immigration and settlement issues, I extensively referred to the A-Z entries and other chapters in James Jupp (general editor), *The Australian People: an encyclopedia of the nation, its people and their origins*, Angus and Robertson, 1988. The second edition of this wonderful encyclopedia will be released as part of the Centenary of Federation celebrations in 2001.

I also found valuable information and insights in James Jupp's smaller publication, *Immigration*, Sydney University Press, 1st edition, 1991, 2nd edition, 1998.

Other general immigration histories spanning the 20th century included:

M Brandle & S Karas, *Multicultural Queensland: The People and Communities of Queensland: A Bicentennial Publication*, Ethnic Communities Council of Queensland and the Queensland Migrant Welcome Association, Australia, 1988

Department of Immigration, Local Government and Ethnic Affairs, *Australia and Immigration, 1788-1988*, AGPS, Canberra, 1988

W A Douglass, *From Italy to Ingham: Italians in North Queensland*, Queensland University Press, 1995

M Dugan & J Szwarc, *Australia's Migrant Experience*, Edward Arnold Australia, Melbourne, 1987

From Many Places: the history and cultural traditions of the people of South Australia, Migration Museum, in association with publisher Wakefield Press, 1995

Immigration Reform Group, *Immigration: Control or Colour Bar?*, MUP, Melbourne 1960

J Lack & J Templeton, *Bold Experiment: A Documentary History of Australian Immigration since 1945*, Oxford University Press, Melbourne, 1995

A number of histories of specific communities were valuable sources of information:

A & T Batrouney, *The Lebanese in Australia*, Australian Ethnic Heritage Series, General Editor, M Cigler, AE Press, Melbourne, 1983

U Beijbom & J S Martin, *The Swedes in Australia, Vol 1- Colonial Australia, 1788-1900*, River Seine Press, Australia, 1988

Bridging Two Worlds: Jews, Italians and Carlton, exhibition text co-written by Arnold Zable, Ilma Martinuzzi O'Brien, Helen Light and Anna Malgorzewicz, Melbourne

C Y Choi, *Chinese Migration and Settlement in Australia*, Sydney University Press, 1975

M M de Lepervanche, *Indians in a White Australia*, George Allen & Unwin, Australia, 1984

A Grassby, *The Spanish in Australia*, Australian Ethnic Heritage Series, AE Press, Melbourne, 1983

P Hill, *The Macedonians in Australia*, Hesperian Press, Western Australia, 1989

K Hvidt & H Otte (eds), *Danish Emigration to Australia*, Danish Society for Emigration History, Denmark, 1988

M Jones (ed), *An Australian Pilgrimage: Muslims in Australia from the Seventeenth Century to the Present*, Victoria Press in association with the Museum of Victoria, 1993

T G Jones, *The Chinese in the Northern Territory*, Northern Territory University Press, Darwin, 1997 (revised edition)

O Koivukangas & J S Martin, *The Scandinavians in Australia*, Australian Ethnic Heritage Series, General Editor, M Cigler, AE Press, Melbourne, 1986

P Macgregor (ed), *Histories of the Chinese in Australasia and the South Pacific*, Proceedings of an international public conference held at the Museum of Chinese Australian History, Melbourne, 8-10 October 1993, Museum of Chinese Australian History, 1995

Fr A Mirzaian, *Armenians: A Pilgrim People in Tierra Australia*, Self-published, Sydney, 1975

M D Prentis, *The Scottish in Australia*, Australian Ethnic Heritage Series, AE Press, Melbourne, 1987

A L Putnins, *Latvians in Australia: Alienation and Assimilation*, ANU Press, Canberra, 1981

N Randazzo & M Cigler, *The Italians in Australia*, Australian Ethnic Heritage Series, AE Press, Melbourne, 1987

R Sussex & J Zubrzycki (eds), *Polish people and culture in Australia*, Australian National University, Canberra, 1985

B York, *The Maltese in Australia*, Australian Ethnic Heritage Series, AE Press, Melbourne, 1986

B York, *Empire and Race: the Maltese in Australia 1881-1949*, New South Wales University Press, Sydney, 1990

Chapters one and two:

D Gibb, *The Making of 'White Australia'*, Victorian Historical Association, Melbourne, 1973

Ian Howie-Willis, *Federation and Australia's Parliamentary System: a pictorial history*, The Parliament of the Commonwealth of Australia, Canberra, 1987. Reprinted 1988.

G Inson, R Ward, *The Glorious Years: of Australia Fair from the Birth of the Bulletin to Versailles*, The Jacaranda Press, 1971

J A La Nauze, *Alfred Deakin: A Biography*, Vols 1& 2, Melbourne University Press, 1965

National Archives of Australia, *Alien Edwardians: Chinese Immigrants and the Commonwealth Government, 1901-1920*

P Stretton and C Finnimore, *How South Australian Aboriginies Lost The Vote, Some Side Effects of Federation*, Old Parliament House Research Paper, Adelaide, 1991

M Willard, *History of the White Australia Policy to 1920*, Melbourne University Press, first printed 1923, reprinted with corrections 1967, reprinted 1974, 1978

A T Yarwood, *Attitudes to Non-European Immigration*, Problems in Australian History, Cassell Australia, 1968

RM Younger, *Australia! Australia! Vol 2, March to Nationhood: a pictorial history*, Rigby, 1977

Chapter three:

C E W Bean, *Official History of Australia in the War of 1914 - 18, Vol 1 (11th edition, 1941) and Vol 11*, by Ernest Scott, (7th edition, 1941), Angus and Robertson, Sydney

Chapter four:

J P Gabbedy, *Group Settlement*, Part 1 & 2, University of Western Australia Press, 1988

M Roe, *Australia, Britain, and Migration, 1915-1940: A Study of Desperate Hopes*, Cambridge University Press, 1995

G Sherington and C Jeffery, Fairbridge: *Empire and Child Migration*, University of Western Australia Press, Nedlands, 1998

M Shmith & D Colville, *Musica Viva Australia – The First Fifty Years*, a Playbill publication, Sydney, 1996

Chapter five:

D Faber, *Origins of an Italo-Australian anarchist. Francesco Fantin in Italy.* Paper presented to the conference on the Italian community in Australia, University of Wollongong, 1988

D Giese, *Courage and Service: Chinese Australians and World War II*, Sydney, 1999

T Kempa (ed), *The Monument of Polish-Australian Brotherhood in Arms*, Hobart, Tasmania, 1984

C Pearl, *The Dunera Scandal*, Angus & Robertson, Sydney, 1983

Chapter six:

R Appleyard, *British Emigration to Australia*, Australian National University, Canberra, 1964

B Collis, *Snowy: the Making of Modern Australia*, Tabletop Press, Canberra, 1990, reprinted with revisions 1998

E Edwards (ed), *Starting Over: Migrants Tell Their Stories*, Self-published, Orange (NSW), 1994

D & M Eysbertse, *Where Waters Meet: the Dutch Migrant Experience*, Erasmus Foundation, Melbourne, 1997

A-M Jordens, *Alien to Citizen: Settling Migrants in Australia 1945-75*, Allen & Unwin in association with the Australian Archives, 1997

A-M Jordens, *Redefining Australians: Immigration, Citizenship and National Identity*, Hale & Iremonger, Sydney, 1995

E F Kunz, *Displaced Persons: Calwell's New Australians*, Australian National University Press, Sydney, 1988

O Lukomskyj, *An Overview of Australian Government Settlement Policy 1945-1992*, Bureau of Immigration Research, 1992

H Martin, *Angels and Arrogant Gods: Migration Officers and Migrants Reminisce 1945-85*, Commonwealth of Australia Government Publishing Service, Canberra, 1989

J Martin, *Refugee Settlers: A Study of Displaced Persons in Australia*, Australian National University, Canberra, 1965

C Murphy, *Boat Load of Dreams: Journeys by European Immigrant workers 1947-1994*, United Trades and Labor Council, Adelaide, 1994

National Inquiry into the Separation of Aboriginal and Torres Strait Islander Children from Their Families, *Bringing Them Home*, Human Rights and Equal Opportunity Commission, Commonwealth of Australia, 1997

M Peel, *Good Times, Hard Times: the past and the future in Elizabeth*, Melbourne University Press, Melbourne, 1995

A Pittarello, *Soup Without Salt: The Australian Catholic Church and the Italian Migrant*, Centre for Migration Studies, Sydney, 1980

N Viviani (ed), *The Abolition of the White Australia Policy: the Immigration Reform Movement Revisited*, Centre for the Study of Australia-Asia Relations, Griffith University, Queensland, 1992

S B Wardrop, *By Proxy: a Study of Italian Proxy Brides in Australia*, Italian Historical Society, CO.AS.IT, Melbourne, 1996

J Wilton & R Bosworth, *Old Worlds and New Australia: the Post-war Migrant Experience*, Penguin Books, 1984

Chapter seven:

Department of Immigration and Multicultural Affairs, *Population Flows: Immigration Aspects*, Commonwealth of Australia, Canberra, 1999

Multicultural Australia: The Next Steps: Towards and Beyond 2000, A Report of the National Multicultural Advisory Council, Vol 1, AGPS, Canberra, 1995

L Jayasuriya & K Pookong, *The Asianisation of Australia?:Some Facts about the Myths*, MUP, Melbourne, 1999

L Jayasuriya, *Immigration and Multiculturalism in Australia: Selected Essays*, School of Social Work and Social Administration, University of Western Australia, reprinted 1999

L Jayasuriya, *Racism, Immigration and the Law: The Australian Experience*, School of Social Work and Social Administration, The University of Western Australia, 1999

L Udo-Ekpo, *The Africans in Australia: Expectations and Shattered Dreams*, Seaview Press, Adelaide, 1999

N Viviani, *The Indochinese in Australia 1975-1995: from burnt boats to barbecues*, Oxford University Press, Melbourne, 1996

Quotations

29
Alfred Deakin
M Willard, *History of the White Australia Policy to 1920*, MUP, 1923, reprinted 1978, p 119

59
C E W Bean, *Official History of Australia in the War of 1914 - 18*, Vol 1, p16

66-7
Statutory declarations by German internees Mitchell Library, State Library of New South Wales, MLMSS261/7 Item 63

121
John Dedman
Australian Archives, *SA D1915/0 Item SA3852 Part 1*

132
Ben Chifley
The Advertiser, circa October 1949

136
Nationalities of Displaced Persons
E Kunz, *Displaced Persons: Calwell's New Australians*, ANU Press, Australia, 1988, p43

161
John Kolkert
In the Steps of Tasman: Dutch Migrant Experience in northern Tasmania, an exhibition at the Community History Museum, Queen Victoria Museum and Art Gallery, Launceston, Tasmania, 1992-3. Oral History Collection tape 1992. OH.48

207
From the Migration Museum exhibition, *Chops and Changes: Food, Immigrants and Culture*, 1996.

298
Arrival Statistics
Commonwealth Bureau of Statistics, *1998 Year Book*

312
Professor Gruen's quotation is taken from his obituary by Max Corden in *The Australian*, 31 October 1997

315
Reproduced with the permission of the Council for Aboriginal Reconciliation

318
Multicultural Australia: The Next Steps: Towards and Beyond 2000, Volume 1, p 4
A Report of the National Multicultural Advisory Council Commonwealth of Australia 1995 Commonwealth of Australia copyright reproduced by permission

Index

THE CHANGING FACE OF AUSTRALIA